THE MIDLAND & SOUTH WESTERN JUNCTION RAILWAY

by

COLIN G. MAGGS

DAVID & CHARLES : NEWTON ABBOT
LONDON NORTH POMFRET (VT)

ISBN 0 7153 7978 X

First published 1967
Revised edition published 1980

Printed in Great Britain
by Redwood Burn Ltd, Trowbridge & Esher
for David & Charles (Publishers) Limited
Brunel House, Newton Abbot, Devon

Published, in the United States of America
by David & Charles Inc
North Pomfret Vermont 05053 USA

Contents

Illustrations

Preface to Second Edition

Since the publication of the first impression of this book in 1967, several changes have taken place. The section of the MSWJ from the junction with the main London–Bristol line at Rushey Platt to Swindon Town enjoyed a brief resurgence of traffic in the early 1970s when used by two daily trains carrying constructional material for the M4, but after the motorway's completion and the closing of Moredon power station, latterly used only at periods of peak load since it had become increasingly uneconomic to run, the track from Moredon to Swindon Town was lifted in 1978.

Thamesdown Council purchased the formation and at the time of writing, interest in the line is growing and the vigorous Swindon & Cricklade Railway Company, incorporated on 13 November 1978, hopes to relay the line between Moredon and Cricklade and form a junction with British Rail's Swindon and Gloucester line north of Moredon. In places the track bed of the MSW has been obliterated by various road improvement schemes, but the formation can still be traced for most of its length and there are still minor relics to be seen by the sharp-sighted, such as a wooden signpost beside the A429 pointing to Foss Cross station.

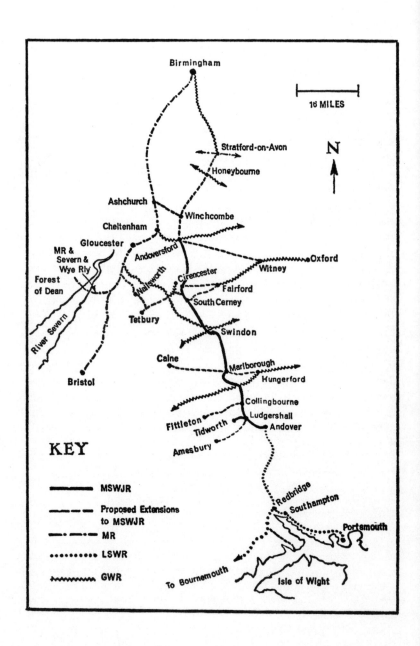

16 MILES

N

Birmingham

Stratford-on-Avon

Honeybourne

Ashchurch

Cheltenham

Winchcombe

Gloucester

MR &
Severn &
Wye Rly

Forest
of Dean

Andoversford

Witney

Oxford

Wallsworth

Cirencester

Fairford

River Severn

Tetbury

South Cerney

Swindon

Bristol

Caine

Marlborough

Hungerford

Collingbourne

Fittleton

Ludgershall

Tidworth

Andover

Amesbury

KEY

━━━━━━ MSWJR

── ── ── Proposed Extensions
to MSWJR

─ · ─ · ─ MR

· · · · · · · LSWR

∿∿∿∿∿∿ GWR

Redbridge

Southampton

Portsmouth

To Bournemouth

Isle of Wight

CHAPTER 1

The Manchester & Southampton Railway

ACROSS THE GRAIN OF TRAFFIC FLOWS

The Midland & South Western Junction Railway was a small cross-country concern with a colourful if chequered history and an individuality which persisted long after the original company lost its independence. Many of its hopes and fears were common to those of other railways built across the grain of traffic flows to and from London; but it also had a fair sprinkling of potentialities and problems peculiar to itself.

It linked Cheltenham with Southampton, though it never reached either of those towns with its own metals. For much of its life it was mainly concerned with the purely local traffic of the downland countryside through which it passed, but for a short spell before the first world war it gained something of the status of a trunk railway route; and in the two wars it carried extremely heavy military as well as ordinary traffic. Most of the system was deep in Great Western territory, yet the MSW by no means always played second fiddle to its big brother. At one time passengers could indeed travel quicker from Cheltenham to London *via* Andover than by the Great Western's own trains. Ultimately, however, the Great Western absorbed the system, and the slow decline began.

In its early days the MSW sported less than three dozen drivers and only twenty stations; everyone knew everyone else and the spirit of comradeship flourished. Nicknames show affection: 'Tiddley Dyke', the 'Humpty Dumpty', 'Neddy's Line'. The company catered conscientiously for its passengers, and was willing to give a personal service of the sort the larger companies could not. It was often ready to stop expresses at intermediate stations to pick up passengers if due notice was given. Goods traffic was enthusiastically canvassed for. But always there was a struggle to make income balance expenditure, and successes such as the routing of Burton-on-Trent beer for Southampton by the line did not compensate for the lack of heavy natural traffic flows in the railway's own territory.

HISTORY IN BRIEF

During the Railway Mania period, 1845, several schemes were proposed for lines linking Manchester and Southampton, but were defeated by lack of finance or by the GWR—jealous of any rivals in the West of England. The idea of a standard-gauge north-to-south railway cutting across the GW's broad-gauge territory remained attractive, however, and after the opening of the Marlborough Railway from Savernake to Marlborough, and the Andover & Red-bridge Railway, a scheme was produced to link these two lines in a Swindon-Southampton route—involving the addition of lines between Marlborough and Swindon and from Savernake to Andover. These connecting links were called the Swindon, Marlborough & Andover Railway. The aims of the Manchester & Southampton Railway would be fulfilled, as traffic from the north could travel to Gloucester, use the Great Western's Cheltenham & Great Western Union Railway to Swindon and then travel onwards to Southampton over the SMA.

The scheme again met with fierce opposition from the Great Western, which disliked the idea of revenue being taken from its northern main line, the Salisbury branch and the Reading-Basingstoke line, and made difficulties which the SMA found hard to overcome. To enable traffic to and from the north to be developed independently of the GWR, the SMA was thus projected northwards as the Swindon & Cheltenham Extension Railway; eventually trains would be able to run to the Midland Railway's station at Cheltenham and provide a direct and easy link between the London & South Western Railway and the Midland Railway, two companies whose relationship was always cordial—warmed by their mutual distrust of the Great Western.

The plan went ahead, but before the line to Cheltenham was opened, the SCE amalgamated with the SMA to form the Midland & South Western Junction Railway. At its inception this line was in grave financial trouble and it remained in the Receiver's hands for many years until Sam Fay took over the general managership and turned the railway into a going, if not very profitable, concern.

To run MSW expresses over the single-track Marlborough Railway was well-nigh impossible as the GWR tried its hardest to be awkward. To avoid difficulties the Marlborough & Grafton Railway was built, at the end of the century, and with its opening the MSW owned an independent stretch of sixty miles from Andover to

Andoversford. Many branches were proposed connecting with the MSW but none came to fruition except the Tidworth Camp Railway. This was the property of the War Office, but was worked by the MSW.

During the first world war the MSW was used by processions of troop trains, ambulance trains, and trains of war materials, being one of the nation's strategic routes, running as it did from north to south. In 1923 it was absorbed by its traditional enemy, the GWR, and no serious effort was made to increase its through traffic. The line was becoming sluggish and drowsy when the second world war gave it a new lease of life and again local people had cause to refer to it as 'the lifeline of the country'.

After the war, lethargy crept in again, and when British Railways diverted passenger trains from Cheltenham Lansdown to Cheltenham St James, the MSW's purpose as a through line was finished. Local traffic was insufficient to make it economic, and most of the route was closed in 1961, though at present two short sections still survive for goods traffic.

EARLY SCHEMES

Trains had started running on the Great Western Railway's main line from London to Bristol, through the northern part of Wiltshire, on 30 June 1841. The Cheltenham & Great Western Union Railway was opened on 12 May 1845, connecting Swindon with the north *via* the Midland Railway at Gloucester. Although this gave a fairly direct connection with the London to Bristol line, its usefulness as a north-to-south route was marred by the famous break of gauge at Gloucester, and also by the fact that even after the goods had been transferred, there was no direct through line to Southampton : an area of 960 square miles was left practically devoid of north-to-south communications.

Traders in Marlborough were left feeling sore, as the coming of the Great Western had stopped the many stage-coaches running between London, Bath and Bristol; and as their profits dwindled they saw their Swindon neighbours becoming more and more prosperous. Wiltshire was an agricultural area, and the advent of the railway had influenced farming; a reduced demand for oats and beans resulted in more land being devoted to green crops.[1]

A rival east-to-west line passing through Marlborough would not have been an economic proposition, but a line from the north passing through Swindon and Marlborough to the south coast would have satisfied the needs of northern industrialists and opened up the county so that more agricultural produce could be sold.

Railway Mania schemes for a north-to-south railway included that for a Salisbury & Swindon Extension Railway to run from Salisbury to Swindon *via* Amesbury and Marlborough. A more ambitious scheme was the South & Midlands Junction Railway, to run from Bicester through Swindon, Marlborough, and Salisbury to Southampton. In Wiltshire, the railway passed west of Marlborough and east of Devizes, both places being served by branches. The West Midland, Manchester & Southampton Railway and the Birmingham, Swindon, Devizes & Salisbury Junction Railway were extensions of the South & Midlands Junction Railway. They were to run from Birmingham through Stratford on Avon, Fairford and Cricklade to make a junction with it at Swindon.

The most promising scheme, however, was the Manchester & Southampton Railway, nicknamed 'Wheeler's Railway', running from Cheltenham to Southampton *via* Cirencester, Marlborough and Andover. The capital was to be £1,500,000 in £20 shares. The M & S scheme was given impetus by the fact that the Midland Railway had snatched the Bristol & Birmingham line from the GWR on 28 January 1845. At a meeting at Southampton on 30 July 1845, the town clerk promised his council's support, and a meeting of the inhabitants on 12 August ratified this.

The M & S was surveyed by Robert Stephenson and he and George P. Bidder were the engineers. The line started at the landward end of the Royal Pier at Southampton and followed the Southampton & Dorchester Railway to Redbridge, three miles away. From there to Romsey and from Timsbury to Leckford it was to be built either on or along the Redbridge & Andover Canal.

It made a junction at Andover with the LSW and at 33 miles 55 chains, by the north end of Collingbourne woods, formed a junction with the proposed Manchester & Poole Railway, then crossing the Kennet & Avon Canal at Wootton Rivers and passing through a tunnel at Savernake. Another tunnel took the railway under the village of Chiseldon. Just before it crossed the GWR east of Swindon Junction, a 20-chain branch led to the station. Beyond North Cerney were three tunnels at Colesbourne and another tunnel under Coberley. The line curved northwards near Cheltenham, joining the MR about 1½ miles north of Cheltenham. At Southampton a tramway was proposed along the waterfront to the dock by the LSW terminus; this would have joined up with the existing LSW tramway to the docks. Apart from the gradient of 1 in 75 up through

Coberley tunnel for trains bound for Southampton, gradients were nowhere steeper than 1 in 100. The whole line would be 88 miles 36 chains long, of which nearly 3¾ miles were to be in tunnels.[2]

Then there was the Manchester & Poole, also with Stephenson and Bidder as engineers. The route ran from the quay at Poole to a junction with the M & S near Ludgershall, a distance of 44 miles 3½ chains from Poole. Another rival was the Manchester, Southampton & Poole Railway, with Joseph Locke as engineer. The proposed terminus was by the swing bridge at Poole Harbour, and its northern end, reached *via* Amesbury, Savernake and Charlton Kings, was to be a junction with the MR near Cheltenham.[3] It had steep gradients and over 3½ miles of tunnelling.

PROGRESS OF THE M & S

The last day for depositing railway plans at the Board of Trade was 30 November, and the vicinity of the offices presented up to midnight a scene of battle and excitement very unusual for a Victorian sabbath. Many railway companies ran special trains carrying plans to the London termini. The *Railway Times*[4] wrote: wrote:

> It is said that the Managing Committee of the Manchester & Southampton and the Manchester & Poole line applied several days before the probable necessity might arise for a special train for Sunday last from London to Southampton in order to ensure in case of need, the due deposit of their plans at more distant places. The public pretty generally know—the public of Southampton to their special sorrow— that, except the Parliamentary train, there is but *one* train on the Sunday morning from London to Southampton, and that such train (doubtless from compunctions of conscience) is four long hours in performing its sacrilegious pilgrimage. The same canons which induced the Managing Committee of the Manchester & Southampton and Manchester & Poole line to ask for a special train, also induces Messrs Hodding and Townsend of Salisbury, acting for the Manchester, Southampton and Poole (known as Lacey's line), and the Salisbury and Yeovil, and other projects to apply for like accommodation. The answer to the Manchester & Southampton Board was an absolute refusal, and this on the sham, and, therefore, shabby ground, that special trains were not allowed, by the South-Western Coy, *unless required by the Government, or upon public service.*
> Messrs Hodding and Townsend, however, it is said, had *three* special trains put at their command; and two of these, if not three, were absolutely used by them in the deposit of their plans—some of which plans, had there not been undue favour, would, we are told, have shared the fate of others of the same party, by being many hours beyond time.

Poetic justice was meted out:

> We rejoice to learn that the line that was, if possible, to be victimized received the lodgement of its plans within the time allowed, and we cannot regret to hear that of the two which it was intended by the South Western to favour, the first was never deposited at all and the second was fatally beyond time.

The M & S bill passed the House of Commons despite severe opposition from the GWR and several landowners; but the Poole scheme was withdrawn in the committee stage. Then the GWR offered to convert its Oxford-Basingstoke line to mixed gauge[5] and this caused the Lords to turn down the M & S bill—by the chairman's casting vote: 'Thus the Upper House rejected a line desired by all the adjoining inhabitants on the ground that public interests would be equally served by a line about 20 miles further away.'[6]

The M & S, not giving up hope, revised its plans slightly for submission to the next session. The junction with the Midland was now to be actually at Cheltenham, modified to connect with the proposed London, Oxford & Cheltenham Railroad. The rest of the route was similar to that proposed the previous year, but with a shortened tunnel south of Swindon and with 305 yd of arching, 45 ft high, at Marlborough over the River Kennet. The tunnel south of the town was shown as not much more than half the length of that in the original plan.[7] Four-and-a-half months later, on 15 April 1847, additional revised cross-sections were deposited, as through the fault of Stephenson the levels were all wrong.

A further M & S plan was deposited on 30 November 1847 for a shortened line from Andover, instead of Southampton, to Cheltenham, and seeking powers for the MR to subscribe.[8] The LSW had earlier that year been granted an Act[9] for building a railway between Southampton and Andover. The shortened M & S was 60 miles 1 furlong 5 chains in length, with modifications to the viaduct and tunnel at Marlborough. But the aftermath of the Railway Mania caused this plan to be rejected too.

Chapter 2

The Railway Takes Shape

THE SWINDON, MARLBOROUGH & ANDOVER RAILWAY

Although the ambitious Manchester & Southampton Railway had apparently failed, the seeds sown by its promoters were still alive and gradually came to fruition. The first of the sections mapped out by the Manchester & Southampton to be actually built was the Marlborough Railway, opened from Savernake on 14 April 1864. This was followed by the opening of the Andover & Redbridge Railway on 6 March 1865. The story of both these lines which became incorporated into the MSW's Cheltenham-Southampton route is told in Chapter 6.

Although they now had access to the GWR's Berks & Hants Extension line, the people of Marlborough still hankered after a line from Swindon to Southampton. In 1864, John Sewell, a London engineer, submitted elaborate reports on the merits of a line called the Gloucester, Wilts & Hants or the Great North & South Junction Railway. He intended using the Midland Railway from the north to Gloucester, the GWR to Swindon and then a new line which would have connected Swindon and Marlborough. From there the existing line, doubled to take extra traffic, would have been used to Savernake and another new line built to Andover. South of the town, running powers over the LSW would be used to Southampton. The proposed capital was £300,000, thought sufficient for building the necessary twenty-eight miles of new double line. Running powers would have amounted to forty-two miles over the GWR and twenty-four over the LSW.

Sewell became carried away with the possibilities of his scheme, claiming in one pamphlet: 'The local, national and international benefits which will flow from this small expenditure can hardly be over-estimated. . . Internationally, the saving in rail mileage from Manchester and South Wales to Le Mans junction, in the heart of France, will be about 200 miles over the London, Dover and Calais route.'

B

In 1871, considering that Southampton was too far inland for modern exigencies, he proposed the Swindon, Southampton & New Forest Railway—which was his original scheme with a branch from Southampton to Stone Point on the Solent, making a total of thirty-six miles of new railway requiring a capital of £400,000. On 25 May 1872 nine landowners and residents, led by Lord Ernest Bruce (a director of the Marlborough Railway) and Ambrose Goddard, met in the Forest Hotel, Savernake, decided to put Sewell's scheme into practice and invited him to become secretary. At Marlborough 'the utmost enthusiasm prevailed', support being promised by 'the owner of the Ailesbury estates and from the influential body of men who form the Council of Marlborough College'.[1] Lord Ernest Bruce remarked that his friend George Hudson told him that the line must be made some day. Sir Daniel Gooch, chairman of the Great Western, presided over the meeting at Swindon in his capacity as one of the MPs for Cricklade. The project received backing from Gloucester timber merchants, and an enthusiastic coal-master of the Forest of Dean said he foresaw thousands of tons of Forest coal being carried to Southampton and Portsmouth. The Severn tunnel, giving a direct run between South Wales and these towns, had of course yet to be built.

The Great Western and the London & South Western Railway who had regarded the line as a kind of war path, actually declared their concurrence in the scheme, while the South Western agreed if need be to widen its existing Andover & Redbridge line to accommodate the extra traffic into Southampton. So astonishing was this announcement that many began to think that a railway millennium was at hand.[2]

The directors of the Marlborough Railway welcomed the scheme. J. C. Townsend, later the company's solicitor, had the wisdom to see that the Great Western would be antagonistic and was against making use of the Marlborough Railway but was overruled by Lord Bruce. Unfortunately, from the very first, the route was not discussed on engineering merits, but on where the landowners wanted it built.

The bill was introduced in Parliament in 1873 and because its promoters had difficulties in raising the Parliamentary deposit, critics thought its chances of success were slight and it passed unopposed, Royal Assent being given on 21 July 1873.[3] The line was in two parts: Railway No. 1, 12 miles 9.4 chains from just east of the GWR station at Swindon to the terminus of the Marlborough Railway at Marlborough, and Railway No. 2, 14 miles 1.3 chains from the Berks & Hants Extension at Savernake to a point 145 yd east of the 67¾ milepost on the LSW, 1½ miles west of Andover. The Act gave running powers over the Marlborough Railway and the BHE between Savernake and the commencement of Railway No. 2 at Wolfhall.

The capital of the SMA was £375,000 with borrowing powers of £125,000; the Marlborough Railway could subscribe up to £25,000. To make running easier, the gradients of the Marlborough Railway were to be reduced from 1 in 75 to 1 in 90 and the section doubled. Powers were given to use the GWR station at Swindon and the LSW station at Andover.

The Act stipulated that the BHE should pay the GWR the cost incurred in building the junction. If part of the BHE to be used by the SMA was broad gauge, provided the SMA gave six months' notice of opening Railway No. 1 to public traffic, the BHE was obliged to lay a third rail, though in fact the BHE and the Marlborough Railway were converted before the SMA was opened. The SMA was given running powers over the BHE, the LSW and the Marlborough Railway.

In the schedule to the SMA Act[4], William Browne and John Gale, two of its promoters, made an agreement with the LSW, which was to pay for doubling the Andover & Redbridge Railway (see Chapter 6) and ease sharp curves if the SMA required, so opening up the long-awaited route to Southampton. There was no actual junction at Abbotts Ann[5] (later Red Post), west of Andover, and the SMA ran parallel with the Salisbury line to Andover station. The SMA was to buy the land for this line and ground for enlarging Andover station and convey it free of cost to the LSW, which would lay down an extra line beside its other two between the junction and Andover, and maintain it at the SMA's expense. The LSW leased it to the SMA at 5 per cent per annum on the cost of the works, which was £23,141. The land became the property of the LSW in 1912 when it was conveyed free of charge under the terms of the 1873 agreement.

Tenders were sought at the end of 1874, but only one was received—from W. & J. Pickering, for £350,390 11s cash—due to the unsettled state of the money market and the dullness of trade generally. Later a few more contractors were persuaded to tender: one came from Caldwell for £328,628 cash, and another from Reed Bros, for £360,000 under conditions of arrangement. William Wright tendered for £344,797 cash or £399,045 in shares and debentures, and this latter offer was accepted on 25 June 1875. The contract stated that the works should be completed in 30 months.

A. L. Goddard at the half-yearly general meeting on 31 July 1875 said that construction had started at a good time as labour was much freer and the iron market at a low ebb. Mr Wright the contractor agreed to pay a dividend of 6 per cent to the shareholders during the period of construction. The first balance sheet, however, did not present a very rosy picture—£5,337 14s 1d received, against an expenditure of £9,169 10s 6d.

A BAD OMEN

It was a beautiful bright day for the ceremony of turning the first sod. Early in the morning of 28 July 1875, flags appeared in all parts of Marlborough, and visitors came in 'vehicles ranging from wagons laden with country folk to the landau of the squire, or drags and breaks which enlivened the roads from Swindon to Andover'.[6] At the ceremony, in a field at Cold Harbour, Meddown, Lord Bruce said the new railway would enable people to attend meets of the Tedworth Hunt and he anticipated 'a good return of profits from those gentlemen who enter into that truly national sport'.[7]

> The spade having been handed over, Lord Bruce turned up the turf, placed it in the barrow and essayed to wheel it off. But an accident, which it is hoped is not ominous to the success of the line, then occurred. After two or three steps, the wheel of the barrow broke down, and all came to grief. With some trouble, the pieces were put together.[8]

Trouble started at once. A 773 yd tunnel was planned to pass through the hill on which Swindon Old Town was built and this, said the *Swindon Advertiser*[9], was a costly blunder. On the tunnel route, heavy compensation would have to be paid for destroying two brickfields and building sites, whereas most of the route the newspaper suggested was over pasture land belonging to the company's chairman.

COST OF THE TUNNEL ROUTE		COST OF THE ROUTE PROPOSED BY *SWINDON ADVERTISER*	
Earthworks—	£	Earthworks—	£
351,000 cu. yd	17,550	176,000 cu. yd	8,800
Tunnel	42,500	Bridges (6)	4,650
Bridges (6)	4,650	Diversion of roads	370
Diversion of roads	370	Contingencies 10%	1,380
Contingencies 15%	9,750		
	74,820		15,200

DIFFERENCE—£59,620

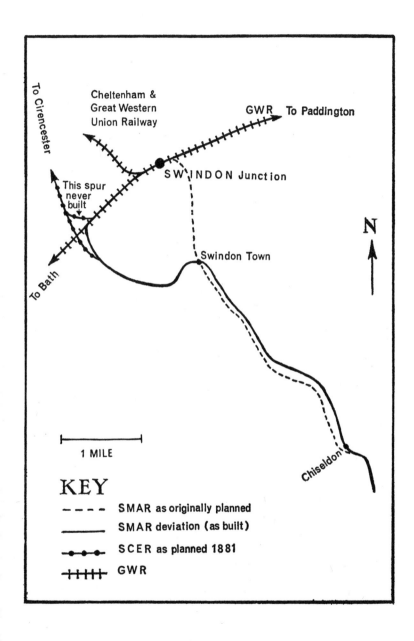

To Cirencester

Cheltenham &
Great Western
Union Railway

GWR To Paddington

SWINDON Junction

This spur
never
built

To Bath

Swindon Town

N

Chiseldon

1 MILE

KEY

- - - - SMAR as originally planned

──── SMAR deviation (as built)

•─•─• SCER as planned 1881

+++++ GWR

Wright started groundwork and clearance for this tunnel, but his progress was unsatisfactory. In November, G. P. Bidder the consulting engineer recommended a deviation between the north end of the tunnel at Swindon and the Bush Inn, just beyond Chiseldon. This modified route had the advantage of more uniform gradients and better station accommodation at Chiseldon. There would also be a saving of about £7,000. But the scheme could not be worked out in detail because of 'extremely wet and tempestuous weather'.

As Wright could not find personal security to give the SMA, he had asked that his material and plant on the ground should be security. Months had passed, but the value of the materials was less than that promised in the contract deed. Then, in December 1875, the company's solicitor reported that work on the tunnel had been stopped as the contractor was unable to pay the men's wages. W. J. Kingsbury, then the SMA engineer, verified that plant to the promised value of £10,000 had not been put on the site and the directors declared the contract null and void. Wright retaliated by threatening proceedings against the company if fresh contracts were signed.

At the half-yearly meeting on 30 August, Gale announced that the directors were in treaty with two or three other contractors. This led to the following letter being sent to the editor of the *Wilts & Gloucestershire Standard.*

> I have this day only read a report in the *Wilts & Gloucestershire Standard* of the 2nd ultimatum, of the half-yearly meeting of the above Company, and as I believe you are desirous of avoiding the insertion of anything in that journal which is calculated to prejudice the public, I beg to inform you that Mr Brooke, the secretary to the Company, has been served with a notice not to enter into any fresh contract for the construction of their line, for the simple reason that the contracts entered into between the directors and myself and bearing the dates respectively the 27th day of July, 1875, and the 19th day of October, 1875, are still in existence, and the proceedings already instituted against the Company will be continued immediately after the long vacation, when, as I am advised by the most eminent counsel, those contracts can be enforced, and should such be the result this will most assuredly be done, and the whole works will be resumed.[10]

Wright never seems to have taken proceedings, however. During the next two years several offers were received from contractors who lacked the necessary financial backing, and the SMA itself went on with the works, even laying a few rails, but finally stopped work in October 1876 when funds ran out. On 9 November 1877, Gooch was asked if the Great Western board would subscribe, but this approach proved fruitless. An Act was duly passed on 16 April 1878 extending the time of completion from 21 July 1878 to 21 July 1881.[11]

By November 1878 the directors realised that there was no hope of receiving the large cash subscription necessary to construct their line, landowners preferring to assist verbally rather than financially. So they proposed a new route, abandoning part of the line and making deviations which they believed would considerably reduce the cost; they felt that a contractor could be found who would take a portion of share capital as part payment. This new route, authorised by an Act of 3 July 1879[12], was similar to that suggested in the *Swindon Advertiser* four years before, and avoided the tunnel at Swindon and a long viaduct at Marlborough. It had the disadvantage of steepening the ascent out of Swindon from 1 in 100 to 1 in 75, and required a separate station at Marlborough as the levels were not suitable for using that of the Marlborough Railway—which it joined 25 chains beyond the station. Another drawback was that the SMA would have to travel 1¼ miles along the GWR to Swindon Junction, instead of a few yards.

In February 1879 Alfred Giles, MP for Southampton, attended a board meeting, offered to construct the line for £200,000 excluding the cost of land and promised to subscribe £50,000 when the public had subscribed the remainder. The directors also promised to subscribe £50,000. Efforts were made to rouse the interest of the Southampton Chamber of Commerce.

At the company's half-yearly meeting on 28 February 1879, the directors said that owing to the continued depression of trade, and the failure of banks and other public companies, they had still been unable to arrange a contract. They sugared the pill by saying that the delay was really a blessing in disguise as iron, steel and other materials were now cheaper as well as labour, so the cost of building the railway would be a third less than that estimated in the Act.

At a meeting at Swindon on 21 August 1879, it was revealed that John Dixon ('Cleopatra's Needle' Dixon, who brought that monument to England) was willing to build the line, provide the capital and pay 5 per cent if the directors and the public would subscribe £60,000; he promised to make the line for £400,000. But this offer was turned down in favour of Watson, Smith, Watson Ltd, whose tender was approved on 29 August 1879. Henry Rose, the company's London solicitor, felt so strongly that Watson, Smith, Watson might suspend operations when the line was partially complete that he resigned, stating in a letter of 18 November 1879[13] that the whole arrangement hangs on the ability and willingness of Messrs Watson, Smith, Watson to fulfill the engagement. Without suggesting any slur on those gentlemen or their financial ability, it will, I presume, be conceded as very improbable that they will be able to find the necessary cash to complete the line without the aid of responsible and powerful backers, and I confess that in the absence of definite information to the contrary, I am unable to see any sufficiently strong inducement either to the South Western or the Midland Railway Companies to back the undertaking even if it were extended westwards to meet the Midland system bearing in mind the existence on the one side of the Somerset & Dorset route and on the other the great probability of the Didcot, Newbury & Andover line being completed.

In spite of this prophecy work proceeded well, and in September 1880 it was hoped to open the line from Swindon to Marlborough by the end of the year. The stations at Swindon, Chiseldon and Ogbourne were being erected by John Dover of Oxford for £4,281. He also built stations at Grafton, Collingbourne, Ludgershall and Weyhill for £2,554. The intermediate stations had crossing loops, but at first only single platforms.

One hitch was a clash with the Marquess of Ailesbury: the line passed near some farm buildings of his, near Collingbourne, and he required the company to take them down and rebuild them on another site because, being so near the railway, they would not be insurable against fire. As removal would have cost £3,000, the SMA decided that a deviation would be cheaper.

A meeting was held in Bridgwater[14] to consider asking the SMA to extend its line to the town, but the local financial position precluded any action and eventually Bridgwater broke the GW monopoly of its traffic by having a branch of the Somerset & Dorset.

OPENING THE SMA

In November 1880 three engines were ordered from Dübs & Co. at £1,600 each, and T. H. Smith was appointed traffic manager for seven years. By June 1881 the Swindon to Marlborough section was nearly completed, and the Mayor of Marlborough, one of the directors, invited the Marquess of Ailesbury and others to run over the line on 25 June. SMA officials began their duties on 1 July. The *Marlborough Times* reported:

In daily expectation of the visit of the Inspector of the Board of Trade, a train service has been running experimentally on this line. Five trains have been started each way, stopping at Chiseldon and Ogbourne stations, and the journey between Marlborough and Old Swindon has in every case been accomplished in 25 minutes. Trains have been

THE SMA—1

(1) *No. 7 at Andover Junction, August* 1913
(2) *Ludgershall from the north, May* 1955

THE SMA—2

(3) *Grafton station looking south.* SR *upper-quadrant signals*

(4) *South portal of Marlborough Tunnel, showing down line lifted,*
February 1965

MARLBOROUGH'S STATIONS

(5) *Marlborough High Level and engine shed. The Low Level station is to the left of the signal box. April 1961*

(6) *Marlborough Low Level from the south, May 1955*

SWINDON TOWN

(7) No. 24 on up line, September 1899

(8) 7824 'Iford Manor' on a down passenger train, and 9600 on the milk train. The former MSW offices can be seen on the right. June 1951

loaded with passengers (primarily from Swindon) for these gratuitous trips, and everything has run smoothly and well.[15]

In fact one mishap did occur, on 11 July, with the train from Swindon to Marlborough. Just before pulling up at Chiseldon, as the guard passed along the footboard to close an open door to prevent it from being damaged by the platform, he slipped and had his foot crushed under a wheel.

Colonel Yolland inspected the line on 20 July, in a train of four coaches drawn by two engines, and suggested several minor improvements. Boarded footways had to be laid at the stations and nameboards erected. Stretcher bars were required at all facing points and he noticed the locks and locking bars were moved by a single lever: 'This is a recent alteration and not an improvement. It will be better and safer to actuate them by separate levers.'[16] And shelter should be placed over the urinals. As the company was willing to co-operate, he recommended that the Board of Trade should pass the line. Colonel Yolland, indeed, paid special tribute to the solidarity of the bridges, mostly constructed with stone abutments and brick arches, or wrought or cast-iron girders. He also commented:

> The connections with the Marlborough Railway have not yet been made, and there is no doubt that arrangements should be made for working into their new station at Marlborough by the Great Western Railway Company which now works the traffic on the Marlborough Railway.[17]

Early on 26 July, two days before the sixth anniversary of the turning of the first sod, a special train carried about eighty boys from Marlborough College home for their holidays; these were the SMA's first fare-paying passengers. (Malburians, of course, soon twisted the railway's name to Turnover Swindle.)

When the first sod had been turned at Marlborough, it had been agreed that, to be fair, the opening celebrations should be held at Swindon. The opening committee travelled from Swindon to Marlborough to meet the Marquess of Ailesbury and the mayor and corporation of Marlborough, boarded a special train which left Marlborough at 2 p.m., and was greeted at Chiseldon by pupils of the village school singing the 'Swindon & Marlborough Railway Song'—composed and set to music locally. For many months this school had had its roll augmented by children from the huts which had been erected to accommodate the workmen's families.[18] The train arrived at Swindon with loud detonations of fog signals.

The gentry proceeded through streets decorated with festoons and bunting, led by the Swindon Town Band in their gay red and blue uniforms, to the inevitable banquet, at the Corn Exchange. In reply to a toast, the vicar of Swindon spoke of 'one blot on their fair escutcheon':

> He was very sorry to see they were going to run two Sunday trains (cheers) which would be giving the people of Swindon additional facilities for desecrating the Sabbath, and he should be glad if they could see their way clear to have written up on their stations before next Sunday, 'No Sunday trading done here'.[19]

It was later pointed out to him that Sunday trains avoided the hours of church services. Regular services began the following day and a handbill announced:

> On and after 27th July, the portion of the line between Swindon and Marlborough will be opened to both passenger and goods traffic and a service of passenger trains will be run at such hours as to meet the principal trains of the Great Western Railway Company, thus affording the most expeditious route between the stations of the Berks & Hants Railway and Swindon, effecting a saving of one to two hours between Marlborough and Bath, Bristol and London, and about three hours to Gloucester, Cheltenham, South Wales etc.

On the railway's first August Bank Holiday, the ordinary train services were suspended and special trains run at intervals of $1\frac{1}{2}$ hours, principally taking people to Savernake Forest for picnics. Of the 1,400 passengers carried, 950 booked from Swindon.

Goods traffic was very light, and was not expected to develop until a connection had been made with the Great Western, but the opening of the railway succeeded in reducing the price of coal at Chiseldon by 5s a ton. Although the Marlborough Railway had to cut its coal rates to compete it found its passenger receipts had increased.

GREAT WESTERN OPPOSITION

The SMA brought its embankment and rails close to the Great Western line at Swindon weeks before the opening, but the GWR, which wanted to put in the junction itself, did not complete it even though the Act gave the new company running powers. People remarked on the different treatment afforded the Swindon and Highworth Light Railway, with which a junction was made long before its rails were ready. The GWR of course had some reason for being obstinate now, threatened as it was with competition between Cheltenham and Southampton—by the Swindon & Cheltenham

Extension, which had just been authorised. The GWR route from Cheltenham to Southampton *via* Basingstoke was 28 miles longer than the MSW's.

Even when the Swindon junction was completed (it was passed by the Board of Trade on 20 October 1881) it lay unused. The dispute was taken to the Railway Commissioners, who on 21 January 1882 said that there had been

> an infringement of the Traffic Act and that this through traffic ought to be forwarded without delay. If this were an application of the traders only against both companies as respondents, we should have no difficulty in making the necessary order, but the fact that one of the companies is an applicant against whom, therefore, no order can be made directly, gives rise to a certain amount of complication.[20]

The Commissioners suggested that the SMA should work into Swindon Junction and interchange there, as it had running powers to do so. This would give the traders the same service as if the GWR exercised its right to carry goods to Swindon Town. As the GWR was the respondent the election of the method rested with it. 'If the Great Western Company shall from one week from this date elect to put into force their running powers, we will make no order on this application.'

An agreement ensued, and SMA passenger trains ran into the GWR's Swindon station on 6 February 1882. The tolls were calculated on a notional distance of six miles from the junction at Rushey Platt to Swindon Junction, instead of the actual distance of 1 mile 18 chains. The GWR demanded a minimum payment of £900 per annum, plus £1,500 for the use of the station, and also a payment of £5,000–£6,000 for an easement for the junction at Rushey Platt. These terms were later reduced by arbitration to a notional distance of two miles, with a minimum of £200 a year for the tolls, £900 for the use of the station and £105 for the junction easement. The service was withdrawn on 28 February 1885 as it was losing the SMA nearly £1,500 a year.

Construction of the southern section continued, and Major Marindin inspected the line on 21 March 1882. At 11 a.m. a special train of two composite coaches, a guard's van and four or five goods vans laden with stores and drawn by No. 4, the Fairlie engine (see Chapter 10), left Swindon. The points and signals of the junction with the GWR at Marlborough were inspected first. Steam was shut off on No. 4 and a Great Western pilot engine put in front for the trip to Wolfhall Junction over the Marlborough branch and the BHE; the greatest care was taken by GWR officials that the Fairlie did not steam over their road as an agreement had not yet been signed. Savernake brought an hour's delay as the junction points had been spiked. Points and bridges on the southern section were tested and Ludgershall reached at 3 p.m. when a stop was made for lunch. A heavy storm of snow and sleet made the inspecting party's position on the front of the engine unpleasant. Andover station was reached just after 6 p.m.

Major Marindin asked for several minor improvements and observed, firstly, that the Marlborough Railway was not provided with block telegraph instruments and was worked with a wooden train staff and ticket.

> Secondly, that at Savernake Station on the Berks & Hants Railway which is used and worked by the Great Western Railway, the arrangements are such as would not be sanctioned upon a new line at the present time and are in many respects faulty. The junction of the Marlborough line with the Berks & Hants line is not properly laid or signalled—there is a want of interlocking of the points and signals and there is only one platform at the station which is used as a passing place so that loaded passenger trains have to be backed from the platform into a loop.
>
> I have therefore to report that although the fulfilment of the few requirements which I have noted as being necessary upon the new line and which have been ordered to be at once attended to, would render these lines, including the junctions at Marlborough and at Wolfhall, in themselves satisfactory, and safe for passenger traffic; yet in that inasmuch as no station has been provided for the reception of traffic at the north end of the Railway No. 2 and the south end of Railway No. 1, except that at Savernake, which is not fit for the existing traffic and still less for the additional traffic which would pass through it upon the opening of the new lines, I must report that by reason of the incompleteness of the works, these new lines cannot be opened for passenger traffic without danger to the public using the same.
>
> In addition to the alterations which are necessary at Savernake Station, block working should be introduced upon the Marlborough line before the through trains from Swindon to Andover can be safely run upon it.[21]

The SMA wrote to the Marlborough Railway offering to carry out at once the necessary alterations on the Marlborough Railway and the BHE. The company preferred to use its own contractors, as plant and material were available and this would be the most economical method; but it was quite willing to pay the GWR if it wished to do the work itself.[22] (The SMA put a section in its 1883 Act saying that the Great Western 'shall forthwith execute, at the expense of the company, all such works as the Board of Trade may require to be executed for the safety of the public'.)

The Marlborough company told the GWR that it thought the SMA's offer eminently satisfactory[23], and hoped the GWR would facilitate a speedy opening; but unknown to the Marlborough Railway, the GWR insisted that the SMA should bear the entire expense of sidings and increased station accommodation at Savernake. The SMA contended that as it was already bound to pay a toll of not less than £300 a year for the use of the station, it was being called upon to pay both the principal and the interest. At a meeting on 20 May, Grierson, the GWR solicitor, suddenly proposed that the matter should be taken before the Board of Trade. The Marlborough Railway, still in the dark, was then startled to receive a letter dated 12 June[24] from the SMA's solicitors saying that the matter was being brought before the Railway Commissioners. The application was heard on 26 July 1882 and dismissed with costs against the SMA, as the Commissioners had no jurisdiction to make an order.

Meanwhile the directors of the SMA had had to decide whether to allow their officials at the various stations between Savernake and Andover to remain unemployed, as some of them had been for over six weeks, or whether they should pick up a few crumbs by opening for local traffic. They decided to open the line from Grafton to Andover. The first train left Grafton at 7.30 a.m. on 1 May. It did not carry many passengers as the traffic was purely local until the gap of 1½ miles was closed, but including the short road journey the distance from Swindon to Andover by rail was shortened by forty miles. The directors and a few officials travelled in the 11.20 a.m. from Grafton to Andover, where they lunched in the Star & Garter before returning.

The single line had stations and crossing loops at Grafton, Collingbourne, Ludgershall and Weyhill. The independent road between Red Post and Andover Junction was not ready and so a temporary connection was put in at Red Post and the LSW line used until 19 November 1882.[25] It was intended to start a through service from Swindon to Andover by running horse brakes or omnibuses between Marlborough and Grafton, but later this was thought inexpedient. As the railway officials themselves had difficulty in travelling between the two sections, however, the traffic manager appealed for a horse and trap to be provided. In the first half of the year, until 30 June, the SMA carried 1,041 first-class passengers, 4,282 second-class, and 43,084 third-class, in addition to 9 season-ticket holders.

Marlborough Railway shareholders, told in September that their dividends were down, asked their directors to see the GWR and urge 'the expediency of pressing on the execution of such works without a day's unnecessary delay'. The law charges in the affair had amounted to nearly 1 per cent on the ordinary shares—the Marlborough Railway was of course paying for the tardiness of the GWR.

The block telegraph was put in on the Marlborough Railway at a cost of £247 12s 4d to the SMA. The secretary of the GWR told the SMA on 9 November 1882 that the Board of Trade requirements for the SMA's use of Savernake station would cost £4,660. The work was carried out and ready for use by 25 December 1882.

In January 1883 the Railway Commissioners heard complaints by the merchants and traders in business at Marlborough, Swindon, Andover and other places that the SMA did not book or work traffic to and from the BHE. The junction at Marlborough was physically complete and it was proved that the only reason why it had not been opened was that the SMA had not given the necessary notice—when given, it would have become liable for the junction expenses. The Commissioners were reported as saying they would have had no difficulty in making an order against the SMA, but the complaint was against the Great Western only, and that company was not responsible.

Traders also grumbled, in support of a supplementary case before the Commissioners, that goods consigned from the GWR *via* the SMA to Marlborough were delivered by the Great Western's route instead. Some GWR stations refused to accept consignments to the SMA line. No case was made out for interference and no order made for costs to the GWR or SMA; costs were awarded against the Marlborough Railway and the BHE—the price for wrongly combining with the SMA against the GW.

The same month saw completion of the works between Marlborough and Wolfhall Junction, and following the Commissioners' ruling, terms were arranged between the SMA and the GWR. Colonel Yolland inspected the junction at Savernake on 31 January and found it satisfactory. At Savernake a down platform had been built, and the land forming the head of the canal tunnel over which the station was built had been taken in for additional sidings.

Invitations were sent out at once for the ceremonial opening on 3 February. Guests left Swindon Town station at 10.40, and their train called at various stations and arrived at Andover at 12.20. There they enjoyed a sumptuous lunch in the Town Hall, costing the SMA £79 15s 4d. The SMA was thus opened throughout from Swindon to Andover on 5 February 1883, and all trains conveyed through coaches to Southampton. The first train was made up of five LSW coaches and a brake van. The *Swindon Advertiser* did not fail to note in its editorial that when the GWR had been the sole railway in a town it

charged the utmost farthing for the accommodation it has afforded; but when there has been competition, when other railway systems have contended with it for the trade and patronage of a town or district, then the Great Western had lowered its rates and extended its facilities in a very marked manner.[26]

CHAPTER 3

Expansion

THE SWINDON & CHELTENHAM EXTENSION RAILWAY

The future of the SMA depended on its use by through north-to-south traffic; without it, a line through the centre of Wiltshire could not hope to be economic. But while the system ended at Swindon, and the GWR had to be used between there and Cheltenham, there was scant chance of prosperity. A few coal trains from South Wales and the Forest of Dean did use the route with its reversal at Swindon, but an independent line to Cheltenham was the first essential.

The Swindon & Cheltenham Extension Railway was planned to run northwards from the SMA at Rushey Platt, Swindon, to Andoversford, on the Banbury & Cheltenham, whose rails would be used into Cheltenham, while there was a proposed branch line running from Cirencester to Fairford and connecting with the East Gloucestershire Railway. In the discussions on the SCE bill, its supporters said that the SMA was an independent little company and should be made sufficiently large to enable it to retain independence. The Great Western, ever jealous of its competitors, tried to stifle the SCE so that it could keep possession of the EGR, and also calculated that the SMA would fall into its hands on its own terms.

Plans for the Swindon end of the SCE were modified in the Commons; Railway No. 3, by which it was proposed to run into Swindon station, was to be used only for interchange traffic. The GWR prepared an enormous plan of the route from north to south designed to show the soundness of the Great Western gradients and the unsuitability of those of the new line. Unfortunately for the GWR, although James Rew Shopland, the SCE's engineer, had not seen the chart before it was hung in front of the Lords, he promptly observed that the gradients were all wrong, containing dozens of errors, a particularly inane one leaving Southampton 243 ft in the air; needless to say, the sketch was not referred to again at the inquiry. One source of support for the SCE was Earl Bathurst, who owned nearly 10,000 acres near Cirencester. He commented on the

NORTH OF SWINDON

(9) *Rushey Platt station signal box, looking south, with the line to Swindon Junction on the left, April 1965*

(10) *Cricklade from the north*

THE SCE—1

(11) *Blunsdon, looking in the up direction, 1935*
(12) *South Cerney & Ashton Keynes station from the south, c.* 1912

impossibility of travelling to Scotland in a day from Cirencester, explaining that the Great Western train connecting with the town arrived at Gloucester one minute after the Midland express had left.

Church bells rang at Cirencester and Cricklade when the bill was passed by the House of Lords Committee, and to mark the occasion the *Wilts & Glos. Standard* published a two-page supplement.

The SCE was incorporated to build a line 27¾ miles long from Swindon to a point just west of the Banbury & Cheltenham Direct Railway station at Andoversford. The BCD was at that time under construction. From Andoversford to Cheltenham, the SCE had running powers over the BCD, GWR and MR. Running powers were also granted over the SMA from Rushey Platt to Old Swindon; over the EGR to Fairford station; and over the GWR to Swindon station. The SCE was to pass under the CGWU, and if it obstructed that line was to pay £50 an hour. The Act was passed on 18 July 1881.[1] The SCE was allowed a capital of £450,000 in £10 shares, with borrowing powers of £150,000. The company had powers to enter into working agreements with the SMA, and the SMA could subscribe, and if necessary raise money for this, by the creation of shares or stock. The SCE was to maintain the line for the first year and the SMA thereafter. On 10 June 1882, C. L. Brooke signed on behalf of both companies, as he was secretary for both.

The first meeting of the directors was held on 25 July 1881. Sir Michael Hicks Beach, MP, was invited to become chairman, but on 13 September he resigned, his views differing from those of the other directors. Watson, Smith, Watson, the SMA's contractors, had their offer to build the line accepted on 25 October. They agreed to pay 6 per cent yearly interest on shares offered up to 31 December 1883, the date fixed for the completion of the railway, and pending the development of traffic to guarantee the dividend of 6 per cent until 31 March 1885.[2]

In April 1882, things began to move. Arrangements were made for the SMA to work the line when completed.[3] At the end of the month the contractors were erecting shedding for their horses at Watermoor, Cirencester. By August nearly all the plant had been delivered and 200 tons of permanent-way materials. The masonry of half the bridges was nearly complete, the junction with the SMA put in[4], and 4½ miles of fencing fixed. Watson, Smith, Watson carried about 120,000 cubic yd of chalk and earth between Chiseldon and Swindon and put in points and crossings at both these SMA stations for working the SCE trains. On 16 July 1883 an Act for a deviation at Cirencester was passed.[5]

C

FURTHER GWR OPPOSITION

Since the opening of the SMA, the GWR had leased the Didcot & Newbury line and was more determined than ever to stop north-to-south opposition. The SCE offered to pay £210 for crossing the Great Western's main line, as the Act permitted it to do, but in November 1882 the GWR asked for, and obtained, an injunction to restrain the small company from entering its land until the capital was fully subscribed; the SCE Act incorporated the Land Clauses Consolidation Act of 1845, which provided that the company should not take land until the whole of the capital was subscribed.

The SCE appealed against the injunction, and on 21 December 1882 the Master of the Rolls, in giving judgment, said the SCE was not taking land compulsorily, and the 16th section of the Land Clauses Act was intended to secure a landowner against having his land taken from him by a railway when there was a probability that the railway would not be made; but here this was not applicable and he reversed the judgment. The GWR went to the lengths of entering an appeal in the House of Lords, but this too was rejected.

Because of their financial difficulties, the SCE and the SMA jointly asked the LSW to work their lines, but this was refused on 3 October 1883.[6] A year later the reason for this was clear: on 21 October 1884 the GWR and the LSW patched up their quarrel and made an agreement to discourage competitive railways in their territories.

In a letter to the SCE on 2 October 1883, the contractor pointed out that the name Swindon & Cheltenham gave potential subscribers the impression of a purely local line; he thought the title one of the principal obstacles in getting capital. An attempt had been made to change it in the 1882-3 session, in the bill for 'the construction of new railways and deviation, additional capital, running powers over a portion of the MR, working agreement with the SMAR and change of name', but this attempt had failed. The only solution was amalgamation with the SMA followed by adoption of a new name for the whole system.

In the meantime, construction work had been going ahead. Rushey Platt platforms were being built at a cost of £250 each and the SMA offered to pay half the cost of the connecting subways.[7] Shopland, the engineer, considered lighting them by gas, the New Swindon Gas Company offering to lay the necessary pipes.

The junction between the SMA and the SCE was inspected by Col F. H. Rich on 9 September 1883; he found that one lever needed interlocking and the permanent way needed repacking. It was re-inspected and passed on 12 October 1883. Goods traffic began between Rushey Platt and Cirencester on 1 November 1883, and Major Marindin inspected this stretch of 13 miles 35 chains on 27 and 28 November. He reported that it was a single line with passing places at Rushey Platt junction station, Cricklade and Cirencester. The works were well and substantially constructed, but on the day of inspection wet weather had caused a slip in the embankment near the Wootton Bassett Road, at the point where the chalk and the clay soils met. Major Marindin would not pass the line for passenger traffic, but goods continued to work over it. Overed Watson, the contractor, said that in the four months from September to December more rain had fallen than for fifty years during the same period. He added that of the opposition, Great Western, landowners and the weather, the last was the worst.

It was calculated that the work on the bank would be finished in eight days, so the opening demonstration was postponed from 5 to 13 December, but numerous engagements prevented the inspector from coming until 17 December. He passed the line, though recommending that the slip should be watched during the winter and trains run cautiously. As the inspection train reached Cricklade, South Cerney and Cirencester stations, bills were posted announcing that the line was passed and would be open to traffic the following day. The inspection train returned over the sixteen miles between Cirencester and Swindon in twenty-two minutes.

Cirencester people had of course arranged a celebration for opening day, but as the rearrangements had been hasty and Christmas was so near, it was postponed until the New Year. However the contractors invited some friends to a champagne luncheon on 18 December. The train carrying the guests left Swindon at 1 p.m. and was welcomed by crowds at Cricklade—the town band playing 'A flower that bloometh'. The following day the Vale of White Horse Foxhounds travelled by train to Swindon for their usual weekly meet at the end of the county.

Unlike Cirencester, Cricklade could not wait until after Christmas and held its celebrations in the White Hart Hotel on the 21st. Sports were held on the following day, with a tea for the children and old people, and a firework display. On 8 January came Cirencester's rejoicings. A public luncheon was held in the King's Head Hotel and the humbler folk filled the market place and played games and sports—jumping, running, bobbing for treacle buns, climbing greasy poles.

THE MSW IS FORMED

By an Act of 23 June 1884[8], the SMA and the SCE were amalgamated to form the Midland & South Western Junction Railway. It was the second railway with this title; the first was incorporated in 1864 and built a line from Cricklewood to Acton Wells Junction and was absorbed by the MR in 1874. The directors of the SMA and the SCE formed the first board of the new railway. The MSW had a working agreement with the LSW to Southampton Docks station and the Act gave powers for making a deviation between Preston and Dowdeswell.

The Swindon, Marlborough & Andover and Swindon & Cheltenham Extension Railway Companies (Amalgamation) Act 23 June 1884 (47 & 48 Vic. cap. lxiv):

| Railway | Capital auth. | | Total |
	Stocks & Shares	Loans	
	£	£	£
SMA	735,000	228,300	963,300
SCE	450,000	150,000	600,000
	1,185,000	378,300	1,563,300

In this 1884 bill, the SCE had sought unsuccessfully for running powers over the GWR from the proposed junction with that company to a junction with the Midland Railway at Standish, south of Gloucester. But the SCE, SMA and GWR made an agreement, dated 17 March 1884, by which the GWR would withdraw its petition to the SCE bill and also the amalgamation bill if the SCE did not seek running powers over its lines. The GWR promised to pay half the cost of the triangular junction with its line at Siddington; expected the SCE to allow it running powers to Fairford; and also expected the SMA's Marlborough to Grafton bill would be withdrawn (see Chapter 4). In addition the GWR promised to do its best to induce the Banbury & Cheltenham to withdraw its opposition to the SMA bill and the amalgamation bill.

Another Act was also granted on 23 June 1884[9], giving powers to make a deviation. It was specially concerned with the protection of the estate of the Rt Hon John Earl of Eldon, and ordered that where the railway was to be constructed on his land in the parish of Chedworth, it must be built as far as possible from the Roman villa on his property. There was to be the minimum of interference with archaeological objects, and 'all such objects whether removed from the surface, or discovered in such excavation shall remain and be the property of the said Earl of Eldon'.

The MSW directors, on 30 June 1884, 'having regard to the present position of the Company's affairs which again received anxious consideration', decided 'to borrow immediately a sum of five or six thousand pounds'. In particular, Beyer Peacock and the Metropolitan Carriage & Wagon Co. were pressing for payment. Economy measures were imperative. To save the extortionate charges paid to the GWR for the use of its line from Rushey Platt to Swindon GWR station, the MSW directors announced that they did not intend working into that station after the expiry on 6 February 1885 of Sir Frederick Bramwell's award of 17 August 1882. C. L. Brooke, the secretary, wrote to the GWR :

> They will be therefore pleased to hear that (with the full knowledge you possess of the heavy loss sustained by this company since it commenced to work into your Swindon station) you will be disposed to make such reductions and alterations in the terms and conditions as will render it possible for this company to continue the use of that Station.

However, the Great Western did not feel inclined to alter the terms.

So serious were the MSW's affairs that the directors convened a meeting of all creditors for sums over £10 at Swindon station on 23 October 1884. One economy was to combine the duties of the general manager and the secretary. On 16 October 1884, Brooke was requested to arrange with Benjamin Lister Fearnley, the general manager since the previous year, to take over his work, and Fearnley was given three months' notice, though he nonetheless stayed with the company until the following year. The Cirencester service was reduced to two trains daily; with the withdrawal of the Swindon Junction service, this allowed a pruning in staff, and also had the advantage of easing the very difficult locomotive situation. No. 3 was in bad condition and receiving repairs, and No. 2 needed repairs as soon as No. 3 was able to work again.

In November, Watson, Smith, Watson, then at work on the Cirencester extension, were released from the contract and went bankrupt the following year.

At the directors' meeting on 27 November 1884 a declaration that the MSW was unable to pay its debts was authorised to be sealed, and another declaration verifying the same was signed by the board before Robert W. Ellett, commissioner for oaths. Both declarations were handed to J. W. Burchall, the company's solicitor. The Hon Mr Justice North made an order on 20 December 1884 that the company's deputy chairman, Lt-Col Francis Douglas Grey, should be appointed the Receiver in Chancery. The company owed £131,647, its debt to its engineer, Shopland, being £13,360, and it had failed to pay interest on debenture stock.

The receiver refused to supply funds to meet the daily loss on passenger trains between Swindon Town and the Great Western station, so these ceased from 1 February 1885. Passenger and parcels traffic for 1883 at Swindon GWR station had produced only £1,635, while the cost of working into and out of that station during the period, including engine power, the proportion of junction expenses, the use of carriages, wagons and station rent, amounted to £3,099 —an absolute loss to the SMA, excluding tolls, of £1,464 8s. The GWR had derived £3,307, or more than double the SMA's proportion of the traffic during the same period. The advice of Archibald Scott, traffic manager of the LSW, and John Morgan, a joint secretary of the London, Chatham & Dover, was sought, and both considered that £300 per annum was sufficient; but the Great Western refused any reduction.

After the MSW service had been withdrawn, the GWR regretted the loss of its toll, and in January 1887 claimed that Sir Frederick Bramwell's award was continuous and that it should still be paid, or that an arbitrator should be appointed. In September, it told the MSW that it intended asking Bramwell for an award of peremptory appointment. The MSW instructed its solicitors, saying it had made repeated proposals and requests, had never received a counter-proposal, and could not agree to the appointment of Sir F. Bramwell although it was quite prepared to go before the Railway Commissioners and accept their decision. There the matter seems to have been dropped.

In April 1885 the Metropolitan Carriage & Wagon Co. threatened to resume possession of the rolling stock unless immediate payment was made; rumour had it that a night watchman had to be kept at Swindon to prevent the threat being put into effect. The directors instructed Shopland to select the most useful items of rolling stock, to the value of the £7,500 which had already been paid, and return the rest.

The same month it was put forward that the MSW should be worked by the LSW, the GWR, or by both companies jointly. In August, the GWR agreed to discuss a working arrangement with a deputation from the MSW, whose board in October recommended that a bill for the GWR working should be promoted in the next session. The terms do not seem to have been satisfactory and nothing more was mentioned about the matter in the minute book.

THE ANDOVERSFORD EXTENSION

Work on the extension to Andoversford (on the Banbury & Cheltenham Railway) was at a standstill, and on 23 May 1887 an Act was obtained giving powers to create debenture stock of £200,000 so that the work could be completed.[10] In January 1888, tenders for the northern section were considered, but none found satisfactory. Rawlence & Squarey, land agents, were informed that the directors had resolved to proceed with the treaties for the purchase of land on the extension and were requested to proceed on the basis of payment in 5 per cent rent charge redeemable by the company after the opening of the line, or if preferred in 'A' debenture stock.

In February, four contractors tendered for the extension and that of Messrs Ridley & Whadcoat was accepted. This contract for construction included the purchase of land and the payment of engineering and other incidental expenses, as well as interest on £189,000 to be paid until the receipt of the Board of Trade certificate. The lump sum of £189,000 was payable in 'A' debenture stock at par on the engineer's certificate. However, before February was out, Whadcoat said that he was unable to accept the tender. Messrs Pearson & Sons and also Mr Ridley asked for the contract, but did not get it.

One contractor, Charles Braddock, was asked if he could amend his tender by £3,000, accepting £188,000 stock and allowing £2,000 for land. On 10 April 1888, Braddock wrote saying he was willing to take £189,000 (amended the following day to £188,000) in 5 per cent perpetual debenture stock. In return he would acquire land for a double railway at a cost not exceeding £15,000 and build earthworks and underbridges for a single line, and tunnel and overbridges for a double line, and pay interest half-yearly on £200,000 debenture stock as issued from the signing of the contract to the completion of the railway. Any saving in costs of construction of the line would be divided, two-thirds going to the company and one-third to the contractor. The following day the MSW accepted his offer.

By early May 1888, a large quantity of plant had already arrived at Cirencester including a locomotive called *Lord Eldon* as a compliment to the nobleman through whose property part of the line was to be built. In June eighteen embankments out of twenty-seven had been formed and about 30,000 cu yd tipped in banks and road approaches. The bridges were progressing well and at Chedworth the gullet at the south end of the tunnel was 30 yd long and that at the north end 60 yd. Men were at work both night and day; 480 navvies, 630 horses, five locomotives and one steam excavator were in use and another steam excavator was being erected.

Lord Eldon proved obstructive, and in July Braddock complained of delay in getting possession of land urgently required for works, but within a month settlements were completed with all the landowners. But next year Lord Eldon claimed £50 damages when his horse fell on a new road the contractors had made at Andoversford. The company suggested that Braddock should be held responsible and not itself, but in the action which followed the MSW had to pay £37 damages. Similar trouble occurred in the spring of 1890, when the Gloucestershire County Council brought a case against the company for having a bad road surface at Andoversford. The company paid ten guineas costs, and offered to repair the road within three months. It debited these costs to the contractor.

On 14 January 1890 the Midland signed an agreement with the MSW allowing the latter access to Cheltenham, and this was followed on 10 April by an agreement with the Cheltenham Station Co. and the MSW for the provision and use of a station at Cheltenham. The Midland Railway was to build a passenger station at High Street, Cheltenham, for £5,410 and a goods station for £2,500, with the land an extra £1,500, the existing Midland Railway Lansdown station being inadequate for the expected exchange traffic. The Cheltenham Station Act was passed on 14 August 1890; two MSW directors promoted the Cheltenham Station Co. which had a capital of £20,000. The MR found most of the money and absorbed it in 1895 (see next chapter).

The contractors duly gave notice of the completion of the line by 24 May 1890 and the Board of Trade was informed accordingly. Booking porters were to be provided at Withington, and the lonely Foss Cross, with a porter and a lad at each; Dowdeswell was to have a stationmaster, two porters and a lad. Shopland suggested that the turntable at Cirencester should be transferred to Dowdeswell and also that a pump be installed there so that it would be a terminus in the event of failure to make satisfactory arrangements for the use of the station at Cheltenham. The company had to bear the expense of maintaining a signal box on the Banbury & Cheltenham Direct Railway at Andoversford at a cost of £180 a year. The committee recommended that the rolling stock the company already owned should work five passenger trains each way plus a goods train. It felt that this was inadequate, but the best that could be done in the circumstances. Three new engines were to be paid for from the return of Parliamentary deposits.

> The present revenue of the opened portion of the line averages £8 5s 0d per mile over 42 miles=£18,000 per annum. When the line is opened, 56 will be this company's mileage and must earn over £12 10s per mile per week to pay the working expenses and five per cent interest on the A Debenture Stock.[11]

TROUBLE AT CHEDWORTH

Early on Monday 9 June 1890, a section of Chedworth tunnel was driven in by pressure of water from a spring. Two lengths of completed brickwork near the Chedworth end collapsed for a distance of about twelve yards and a wedge of earth fell into the tunnel. The slip affected 60 ft depth of earth between the top of the tunnel and the surface of the ground and a hole was formed some yards in length on the slope of the hill above the tunnel.

The contractor did not repair the tunnel and the opinion of a Queen's Counsel was taken as to whether neglect or refusal was a breach of contract sufficient to justify the company taking the work out of his hands. Counsel advised that the engineer should serve on him notice for repairs and completion of construction. The contractor removed one engine and two wagons and an application was made to restrain him from removing further plant. He had also not paid the interest: demand for this was made personally and the tunnel notice sent by registered post. He was given fourteen days to comply, but although he had 120 to 130 men at work, he did nothing towards the repair of the fall.

In July, A. F. R. Daniel, the secretary, who had replaced C. L. Brooke in May 1885, sent a letter to debenture stockholders, saying:

> Owing to the non-completion of the line by the expected date, there is not sufficient in the hands of the Trustees to pay a full Half-year's Interest on the Company's A Debenture Stock due 30th June last, but a demand has been made on the contractors, under his guarantee, for which the company hold ample security available on the opening of the line, for the deficiency.

In September, Charles Braddock wrote a long letter to the editor of the *North Wilts Herald* taking exception to certain of the statements made by the chairman and engineer at the half-yearly meeting; he explained that the delay in completing the Andoversford extension was not due to any fault of his (under the contract it should have been ready by 24 August), but had been caused by Chedworth tunnel falling in.

Early in September about fourteen men were at work on the tunnel and ten elsewhere. The shaft of the tunnel slip had been carried down to the top of the tunnel arch and the top heading along the tunnel had commenced. Shopland pressed for more. On 1 November he reported that the second length of tunnel arch as restored had been turned, that one further length of about 9 ft remained to be turned and that repairs to the unbroken part of the tunnel would have to be made. A fortnight later, the broken arch of the tunnel had been completely restored and the men were taking down the tunnel roof at both ends of the damaged portion, as it had been badly shaken. At the southern end of the tunnel, water had proved troublesome. Shopland thought that repairs would be completed within a month and the tunnel ready for inspection by the Board of Trade. However, a month later the work was expected to take at least another month. The contractor had still not paid the interest, or that due for the new half-year.

At last the work was complete and Major Marindin inspected the line between Cirencester and Andoversford on 23 and 24 January, recommending that this section be opened as soon as the undertaking as to mode of working was received. Between Cirencester and Dowdeswell the line was single, except for passing loops at Foss Cross, Withington and Dowdeswell. At Dowdeswell the line was double for 57 chains before it joined the Banbury & Cheltenham. The overbridges and tunnel were constructed for double line. The junction at Dowdeswell was not inspected as the Great Western would not allow points and crossings to be put in until working arrangements had been concluded. Marindin commented: 'I trust that for the convenience of the public this arrangement may speedily be made.'

FURTHER TROUBLE

About three weeks after the inspection, a serious slip in the embankment at Chedworth weakened an accommodation bridge so badly that it had to be rebuilt; Marindin had warned the company that this embankment should be watched. His inspection had been made at the beginning of a rapid thaw after a protracted frost, and the slip, stretching for 120 yd, in fact started the day after his visit. The line at this point was carried on a low embankment along the east slope of a hill which bore traces of old slips in several places. The top layer of the clay soil, to a depth of eight to ten feet, had been squeezed out by the weight of the embankment and had slid down the side of the hill. The bridge was shored up and the permanent way laid on longitudinal timber baulks. Marindin suggested that a watchman should always be kept on duty at the spot and trains limited to 5 m.p.h. He also inspected the junction at Andoversford, ready except for connecting the points to the signal box.

The Board of Trade sanctioned the opening of the line on 11 March, but snow blocked the whole length. Shopland had the southern section clear the following day and hoped to have the northern section clear by the 13th, but it was not until 16 March that a train carried the directors, secretary and traffic manager from Andover to Cheltenham, and the line opened to goods traffic with three trains each way.

The company gave an excellent service—goods collected in London overnight were ready for delivery early next morning in Cirencester and Cheltenham. Until High Street Cheltenham goods station was ready, two goods trains ran daily from Andover Junction to Dowdeswell. The *Cheltenham Free Press* commented: '1891 will see accomplished what in 1845 Parliament was asked to permit.'

But the financial situation was still far from good and the *Railway Times* said:

> Of £9,907 gross revenue for the last half-year, only £78 was net profit, and ranking before the £110,630 of ordinary shares, there is a trifle of £1,178,497 debenture preference stocks &c. The directors report with 'satisfaction' that the northern extension to Andoversford has been completed and will shortly be opened for passenger traffic. It is satisfactory to find that there exist some people who can find 'satisfaction' in anything connected with this concern.[12]

On 16 May 1891, the MSW signed an agreement with the Banbury & Cheltenham and the GWR regarding 'conditions of user of the Banbury & Cheltenham Railway'. But the through passenger working was held up until facilities at Cheltenham Lansdown station were completed. On 30 June 1891, the MSW ran an excursion from Marlborough to Birmingham and church choirs of Cirencester and district took advantage of this for their outing. This, the first through passenger train over the completed section, carried over 400 passengers. Then, in July, the MR sent a telegram : 'If you can arrange to work your engines without turning at Cheltenham the rest of the work will be ready for opening on the first proximo' (1 August).

The MSW, expecting more through traffic *via* Cheltenham and less *via* Swindon, told the GWR that on and after 1 August 1891 it would cease running into Swindon Junction station and no longer pay the expenses of Rushey Platt Junction signal box; all traffic would be exchanged at Rushey Platt sidings.

THE REST OF THE SYSTEM

Meanwhile, at the other end of the line, on 29 October 1887 the MSW signed an agreement with the LSW regarding terms for the use of Andover Junction station and the line to Red Post. The MSW was to pay a yearly rental of £1,500 and in return the LSW would provide staff for the station and maintain the line to Red Post. A toll of two miles was deducted by the Railway Clearing House from the MSW proportion of receipts and was credited monthly to the LSW as security for the payment of £1,500. The earnings of the line and net terminals afterwards were to be repaid by the LSW to the MSW half yearly.

Delays at Marlborough station were constant, and in December 1887 the MSW asked the GWR if trains could cross at Savernake. This spurred the company to rethinking about building an independent line between Marlborough and Grafton. In February 1888 it proposed that the Great Western be credited with the mileage proportion of through rates and fares for its portion of line, arranged so that the sum credited for the line between Wolfhall Junction and Savernake station was not less than £300 per annum. The MSW agreed to pay the GWR a proportion of the working expenses of Savernake station based on the relative number of trains of each company using the station, and also the expense of the junctions at Wolfhall and Marlborough.

Running expenses were a constant worry. In May 1890, Shopland said that 1,000 sleepers were required (he got them at 4s each) for renewals between Swindon and Andover, and two engines needed repairs which would cost £500 and £300. One of the minor expenses—£1 15s monthly—was pruned when the directors stopped exhibiting large poster time-bills at Bath, Bristol, Cheltenham, Hereford, Stroud and Gloucester. And a new source of income was tapped when in June 1887 the Sweetmeat Automatic Delivery Company offered 25 per cent of receipts, with a minimum of £3 per annum, for permission to stand their machines at MSW stations; these terms were soon changed and two years later the company withdrew its apparently uneconomic service.

In making an effort to gain more through traffic T. H. Smith, the traffic manager, was asked to spend two days in Southampton; he advised also that a cartage agency should be opened at Portsmouth. Some regular mail work was done: in September 1882 the Swindon postmaster had asked what the cost would be for conveying a mail bag once daily for six days a week between Swindon GWR station and Marlborough. The SMA said 6s, providing that the weight was not over 14 lb. In January 1884 the secretary of the GPO asked if the company possessed the necessary facilities and was willing to undertake the collection and delivery of telegrams at Collingbourne Ducis and to transmit them to and from the company's station at Marlborough, where a 'handing-over' circuit to Marlborough post office would be provided. The SMA had agreed. Then, in September 1884, T. H. Smith proposed running a mail each morning and evening between Swindon and Cirencester. The GPO required trains to run to Swindon GWR station, or the bags to be carried from Swindon Town to the GWR station. The annual charge must include that for transferring the bags between Cirencester and Cricklade stations and the respective post offices. The GPO also required the use of other trains. The MSW accepted.

STAFF

For the sake of economy, throughout most of the Midland & South Western's history the posts of general manager and traffic manager were combined, sometimes including even the secretary-ship as well.

T. Harrison Smith was traffic manager from 1880 to 1892. His contract in fact expired in August 1887, when he wrote offering to continue his services at a lower salary, evidently thinking this preferable to having no job at all. J. F. R. Daniel, the general manager, agreed to keep him on at £276 as a temporary arrangement; his former salary had been £400 p.a. Daniel took over as general manager from Benjamin Lister Fearnley (in office 1885-6), holding the post until 1892. The secretary of the SMA and the SCE (the MSW from 1884) from 1873-85 was C. L. Brooke, whose post A. F. R. Daniel (brother of J. F. R. Daniel) took over until the arrival of Sam Fay in 1892.

The SMA's first consulting engineer, G. P. Bidder, died in 1878 before construction had started in earnest. He was succeeded by W. J. Kingsbury on the SMA and Charles Liddell on the SCE. James Rew Shopland was appointed resident engineer to the SMA in 1875, remaining with the MSW until his death in 1897. Shopland also became the company's locomotive and carriage superintendent in 1885, his salary being £600. Fay, soon after his arrival, reduced this to £200, making Shopland a consulting engineer, as a temporary economy measure. Until then the company had owned few locomotives, and their supervision had come under the engineer or general manager.

The usual small staff crises of course arose from time to time. A reshuffle involving four men in September 1884 was the result of the stationmaster at Chiseldon having been absent from duty on two days, and consequently being dismissed. The stationmaster at Ludgershall, then an unimportant station, was transferred to Chiseldon at 23s 1d a week; the Ogbourne stationmaster went to Ludgershall at 21s a week; and the signalman at Chiseldon, who reported the erring stationmaster, was appointed stationmaster at Ogbourne at 18s a week. Then Inspector John Davis was absent from duty and was reduced to the grade of goods and supplementary guard at 20s a week, though a month later, when the stationmaster at Grafton was ill, Davis had to be put in temporary charge as no other suitably qualified employee was available.

The stationmaster at Weyhill was careless and did not properly attend to his duties, so was given a month's notice from 1 January 1885. On 15 January the same year, a driver ran past a stop signal and facing points at Collingbourne and was fined 30s; a signalman was fined one day's pay and the stationmaster three days' pay and directed to receive a severe reprimand. In 1889 the stationmaster at Grafton absconded with £30 takings and a warrant was issued for his arrest. He was never caught and the money was repaid to the MSW by the Guarantee Association of which it was a member. About the same date the accounts of the Marlborough stationmaster also showed a deficit of about £45. The Board's decision that from 1 January 1888 the remuneration of gatekeepers should be reduced to 2s 6d a week must have been received as a bitter little pill.

CHAPTER 4

Consolidation

SAM FAY TAKES CHARGE

Before the line was open throughout from Cheltenham to Andover, this letter was received:

London & South Western Railway,
Traffic Superintendent's Office,
Waterloo Station.
London. Feby. 11th, 1891

Dear Mr Batten,

With reference to our conversation last evening upon the subject of the Managership of the Midland and South Western Junction Railway, I see no reason why the Line should not be worked somewhat upon the same principle as the several districts into which, for traffic purposes, the South Western and all other large railways are divided.

That is to say the Manager would have under him for traffic business, one uniform inspector whose duties would embrace a general supervision of the staff, the signalling arrangements and any other outdoor duties that may be found him. For the loco and carriage and the maintenance of the permanent way, two practical foremen—one for each department—acting under the instructions of the Manager would be needed, but I do not consider a highly paid professional engineer is requisite seeing that no large construction of stock or of way and works is contemplated.

If the Secretarial duties are added to those of the Manager, and I should be quite prepared to undertake this if so required, one clerk should be allotted to this branch of work, and probably one of those now employed under Mr Daniel could do this without any additional cost.

Upon this basis I estimate the expenditure for the executive as under viz.:

Uniform Inspector	30/- per week
Loco Foreman	45/- per week
P.W. „	45/- per week

or a total of £312 per annum exclusive of the salary of the Manager.

I should not like to pin myself absolutely to these figures as there may be local circumstances to warrant a variation either way and this must be taken simply as a sketch of what might be fairly looked upon as the probable cost of management upon the lines which I have indicated.

With regard to the clerical staff, in the absence of detailed information as to the number and material of which it is composed I cannot, of course, form an idea of what may be required, but there is no reason as far as I am aware for increased cost in that direction.

As explained yesterday, I am well acquainted with the character of the district through which the railway runs and also with the towns on the line to and from which your traffic must of necessity flow. If anyone can make it a paying concern, I believe such can be done by

Yours faithfully,
(signed)   S. Fay.

J. W. Batten, Esq.
3 Harcourt Buildings, Temple.

However, at the directors' meeting on 19 February 1891, Lt-Col Grey reported that the proposed appointment had been dropped.

Eleven months later, on 13 January 1892, Col Grey, as Receiver, called a meeting of the managers. The outcome was that a change of management would be made throughout the company and notice was given to all its salaried officers. A representative saw Charles Scotter, traffic manager of the London & South Western Railway, and this resulted in Fay being appointed general manager for a period of five years from 1 February 1892. He was granted a fixed annual salary of £300, with an additional payment of £100 for every £2,000 of net revenue. The MSW made a new agreement with Fay from 1 July 1895, when he was given a contract at £300 per annum and a commission of £5 per cent on any balance to the credit of 'Revenue Account No. 9'.

Letter from Sam Fay to stationmaster at Rushey Platt

THE SCE—2

(13) 31808 *leaving Cirencester with the 1.52 p.m. Cheltenham St James—Southampton train, May 1960*

(14) *Withington, the up road only in use, May 1960*

TWO SMALL SCE STATIONS

(15) *Foss Cross, looking north*
(16) *Chedworth, looking north*

E. T. Lawrence, the secretary, met Fay off the train when he came to take up his appointment as manager. He said, 'Do you know this line is nearly bankrupt and there is not enough money in the bank to pay the staff at the end of the week?' Fay replied, 'Don't say that, I see great possibilities in this line'. He added that he intended to go out in every way to build up traffic.

In some weeks the financial position was so bad that Fay had indeed to go out, going himself to the stations and various debtors to collect enough money to pay the wages. Economies had to be his first concern. He promptly sold No. 4 engine, which had given much trouble, together with all useless stock, and reduced the company's total estimated expenditure by £2,974; he also obtained a cheaper supply of coal, at 14s 11½d a ton. And, as mentioned earlier, Shopland's salary was reduced.

A positive measure was to get more money from advertisement hoardings. As long ago as June 1883, W. H. Smith & Son had offered to take advertising space at the SMA stations and promised to pay to the railway company half the money received for exhibiting the placards, but in return the firm required free transport for the advertisements and free passes for its employees engaged in putting them up. The arrangement was made for five years from 1 July 1883. In 1888 W. H. Smith & Son paid £3 a year for being allowed to advertise on the bridge at Watermoor, Cirencester. In May 1892, Fay arranged for Smith's to pay about £110 a year for advertising. In August 1899, the same company signed a contract for advertising at stations, in coaches and bookstalls for £125 for two years and £150 subsequently. In 1893, Fay booked Walter Hill & Co. to canvass for advertisements to be placed in the company's coaches and in the timetable.

A more important financial measure was, with the consent of the Court of Chancery, to secure a loan of £56,000 for a rolling-stock fund—see Chapter 10 for details. Nicholson Browne, the chairman, reported that this agreement was sealed in June 1896; new rolling stock was bought, both goods and passenger, and a goods engine and two mixed-traffic engines.

On 28 February 1893 the Board decided to instruct its solicitors to take whatever proceedings were necessary to obtain the removal of Lt-Col Grey from the Receivership. He was given £3,000 and forcibly retired from his office in April, Fay being appointed in his place without any remuneration; this appointment was ratified by an Order of the Court of Chancery dated 8 August 1893.

In May 1895, Fay made an agreement with Earl Bathurst and

D

others for a loan of £14,000 and part of it was paid to the creditors of the company. An indication of the company's poverty was that in January the previous year Fay had had to ask for money to have broken windows in stations and offices mended, and he was authorised to spend £200 out of the proceeds of the sales of surplus lands for repairs to coaches. And at the half-yearly meeting on 28 August 1895, a shareholder said the fences from Andover to Savernake were in 'a ruinous condition' and completely down in places; the stations needed paint and repair and at some the line was a mass of weeds.

THROUGH TRAFFIC BEGINS

From 1 May 1892 two MSW engines and trains ran from Southampton to Cheltenham. The LSW made no charge for the use of Southampton Town station under Section 34 of the SMA Act of 1882 and Clause 4 of the agreement with the LSW dated 15 August 1882. Regarding running powers to Southampton, the MSW received as working expenses 25 per cent on passenger traffic and 33 per cent on goods. From 1 June, Burton beer for export and consumption at Portsmouth travelled *via* the MSW in the 7.40 a.m. mixed train from Cheltenham.

By an Act of 6 July 1895 the Cheltenham Station Co. was transferred to the Midland Railway and a new agreement made with the MSW for running powers from Lansdown Junction to High Street and also for the use of Lansdown station by passenger trains. The rent, easement, cost of water, etc for the use of Lansdown worked out at £1,570 10s 10d a year : working expenses were to be proportional to the number of passengers booked by each company. Goods trains from High Street to Lansdown Junction would pay the MR as if for two miles.

OUT OF CHANCERY

The twenty-seventh of May 1897 was a red-letter day in the MSW's affairs. It was resolved that the company should be taken out of the Court of Chancery, where it had been for the last thirteen-and-a-half years, and the Receiver discharged at the earliest possible moment. He was actually discharged by the Court on 10 November 1897, subject to the passing of his final account. Between 1894 and 1898 traffic receipts increased 73 per cent with only 18 per cent increase in expenditure and most of the credit for this was due to Sam Fay.

THE MARLBOROUGH & GRAFTON RAILWAY IS MOOTED

To have two companies working over the single-line Marlborough Railway had never been satisfactory, especially as traffic had grown to such proportions that on average one train was running every twenty-five minutes. The Parliamentary Committee discussing the MGR bill was astonished when Fay showed that within eighteen months to two years 170 trains had been delayed for about half an hour, and one train had been delayed for no less than five hours.

Another disadvantage to the public arising from the arrangement was that the MSW was not allowed to book passengers between Marlborough and Savernake and vice versa; a person travelling between these places by an MSW train had to book from Marlborough to Grafton, or from Savernake to Ogbourne, depending on his direction. The GWR was allowed to veto the MSW's freight rates over this section too.

As early as October 1883[1] the directors of the SMA had foreseen that the Marlborough Railway would be insufficient for the traffic it would carry and had asked the Marlborough directors to discuss doubling it, with reference to the SMA Act of 1873. The two sets of directors met at the Westminster Palace Hotel on 1 November 1883. The following day C. L. Brooke wrote to the Marlborough Railway proposing an additional track beside the Marlborough Railway to within a quarter of a mile of Savernake station where the new line would cross the Berks & Hants Railway and the Kennet & Avon Canal a short distance east of the present bridge at Wolfhall Junction.

> The proposed line from Marlborough Junction of this Company's line to the point about a quarter of a mile north of Savernake Station will be laid in places at improved grades, and when completed used jointly until such time as the present existing line and levels can be altered so that the line between the points named can be used by both Companies as a double line of Railway.[2]

The SMA duly applied to Parliament to double the Marlborough Railway but after the Marlborough Railway directors had seen the Great Western board, it had been pointed out that the additional rail would cost about £75,000, and that the suggested terms were not generous enough, the SMA withdrew—in March 1884—on condition that the Great Western withdrew its petition against the SCE bill.

But the idea was not forgotten, and in October 1888, in spite of

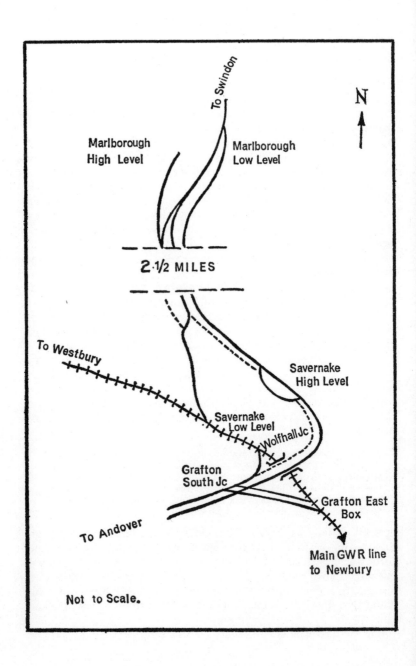

To Swindon

Marlborough High Level

Marlborough Low Level

N

2·½ MILES

To Westbury

Savernake High Level

Savernake Low Level

Wolfhall Jc

Grafton South Jc

Grafton East Box

To Andover

Main GWR line to Newbury

Not to Scale.

the heavy financial commitment of the extension from Cirencester to Andoversford, the MSW instructed Shopland to survey a new line from Marlborough to Grafton. Separate capital would have to be found for its construction as the MSW, being in Chancery, could not raise money for a further undertaking. On 30 November 1888, plans were deposited for a railway with a ruling gradient of 1 in 80 to run from Marlborough to Wolfhall.[3] The GWR, worried about losing tolls of £4,000 a year on the Marlborough Railway, was a very real threat to the proposed line, and there were also petitions in Parliament against it by the East Gloucestershire Railway, Cheltenham Corporation, Lord Eldon, the LSW, the MR, the GWR and the Marlborough Railway. The MSW directors thought the first three opponents would fail, or else be settled: granting running powers would pacify the LSW; the Midland Railway could be talked round; but the GW and Marlborough Railway would have to be fought. For its part, the Marlborough Railway conceded that if the new railway was dropped, it or the Great Western would double the line from Marlborough to Savernake if and when the MSW came to double the Swindon to Marlborough line, the MSW paying 8 per cent for construction or maintenance of the loop or double line, this interest to be reduced or even extinguished with increased traffic.

The matter again fell into abeyance, but delays on the single line continued. In May 1893, Sam Fay complained to the Marlborough Railway of the ways in which its tenants, the GWR, hindered traffic. The Marlborough directors claimed ignorance of such matters and asked for details. Fay replied that his directors 'supposed that your line of Railway was used by the Directors and that therefore they must have been conversant with the delays which so frequently take place'.[4] Fay in due course gave some examples of delays which occurred in June 1893.

> On Thursday 8th instant, a special train with potatoes from Southampton to Birmingham which reached Savernake at 11.20 a.m. was delayed until 12.15 p.m. and subsequently incurred another delay of 1 hour 35 minutes on the Great Western Company's line near Cheltenham.
>
> On the same day, the 3 p.m. passenger train, Cheltenham to Southampton, after being delayed six minutes on the Great Western Company's line near Cheltenham by a goods train in front, was stopped five minutes at Marlborough waiting the arrival of the GW Coy's train.
>
> All trains are delayed at Savernake for the examination of tickets although this Company is as much interested in seeing that Passengers pay their fares as the GW Coy.

Fay also gave an instance of the Great Western veto of reasonable rates.

On April 3rd 1891 a quotation was asked for a rate for bricks between Cosham and Swindon, and 6/8 per ton proposed to the GW Coy, which was reasonable and fair, and was approved by the South Western Company. Correspondence was carried on until July when the GW Coy objected to less than 7/1 per ton being charged although they had been conveying bricks from Stratford on Avon to Swindon for 5/10 per ton, a distance of 82 miles as against 75 miles between Cosham and Swindon. It was not until the Autumn of last year (1892) that these bricks, some 20 tons. were charged up and this Company received their proportion upon them.[5]

In the summer of 1894 another proposal was made for building an independent route from Marlborough to Grafton, but was postponed. Fay said that 'it was impossible to get trains of ordinary weight over the steep gradients of the Marlborough Railway'.

THE MARLBOROUGH & GRAFTON FINISHED

The following year the Marlborough & Grafton Railway was promoted, with Shopland as engineer and Sam Fay as secretary. As the MSW was still in the Receiver's hands, it still could not raise capital itself. The first meeting of the MGR was held at the Junction Hotel, Andover, on 17 September 1895. Shopland reported that he had gone over the route with E. B. Merriman, Lord Ailesbury's steward, and its course had been agreed, except for a slight alteration where the land was owned by St John's college.

In December a provisional draft agreement was made between MGR and MSW. For the perpetual lease, an annual rent of £3,500 was payable, the MGR receiving receipts arising from local traffic, less 25 per cent which would be retained by the MSW for working expenses. The estimated cost of the line was not to exceed £100,000. A schedule to the Act took the form of an agreement between the MGR and the MSW for a perpetual lease of the new line. Ellett, the MGR solicitor, was asked to look into the advisability of asking for a Board of Trade order, instead of applying for an Act, in view of the fact that only Ailesbury property would be taken. The MSW incidentally had the support of the War Office, which was planning to build barracks at Ludgershall and Tidworth on Salisbury Plain and welcomed any scheme which would improve the rail facilities to the district.

The company was incorporated on 7 August 1896[6] and allowed a capital of £100,000 in £10 shares with borrowing powers of £33,000. The Act stipulated that the company should pay the Great Western reasonable expenses for inspecting and watching works

during the making of the new railway over the GWR and the Kennet
& Avon Canal. If works impeded trains, the MSW had to pay £20
an hour, or £10 a day for halting canal traffic. As one of Lord
Ailesbury's fields was cut in half, a pond had to be built for his
cattle to drink from. It was stipulated that land by Wolfhall
Junction was not to be used for sidings or general shunting purposes
during his Lordship's tenancy, and the MSW and the LSW were to
have running powers over the MGR.

Scheduled to the Act was a memorandum of an agreement made
on 27 April 1896 between the provisional directors of the MGR (who
included a representative from the Southampton Chamber of
Commerce—thoughts were still running to a Manchester & Southampton Railway) and Samuel Fay, Receiver and secretary of the
MSW. The MGR was to maintain the line for the first twelve months
and the MSW thereafter. Fifty per cent of the income of the MGR
was to be retained by the MSW.

The powers were for a double track from the junction with the
existing line, 250 yd south-west of Marlborough station, through a
647 yd tunnel, descending the hillside above the Great Western
Savernake station, then crossing the Great Western and the Kennet
& Avon Canal and joining the southern section of the MSW 30
chains south of Wolfhall Junction on the GWR main line. The
gradients were easier than on the old Marlborough branch. The
existing single line onwards to Grafton was to be given to the MGR
and doubled, making the new railway 6¾ miles long. A new station
was to be built at Savernake, 200 yd north of the one belonging to
the GWR.

The board considered two tenders on 14 August 1896. Messrs
Firbank's was for £82,030, the charges to be £2,000 less if chalk
ballast was used. Lucas & Aird submitted a tender for £79,000 and
offered to pay the MSW £1,000 more for conveying stone than did
Firbank. Lucas & Aird's tender was accepted.

Work began in August 1896, almost immediately after the bill
had received Royal Assent. Much local interest was shown in the
marking out of Marlborough tunnel, whose first shaft was started
on 21 October. So precise were the measurements that when the
two headings met in the beginning of March 1897, after five months'
work, it was found that no deviation of more than ⅜ in. had been
made in the whole distance.[7] The headings were then enlarged to
double-line size—25 ft wide at rail level and 20 ft 8 in. high above
the rails. The lining consisted of four rings of brick giving a thick-
ness of 18 in., which was strengthened to six rings at the ends where

the weight of the surrounding material fell. The 2,500,000 bricks required were made at the Malago Works, Bristol. (For subsequent history, see Chapter 8.)

A steam navvy capable of excavating 750 cu. yd daily was used in the cutting at the south end of the tunnel which passed through chalk, dry, light and easy to work. A steam navvy also excavated the bulk of the cutting between Hatt Gate and Leigh Hill; 50,000 cu. yd of material were taken from there to the embankment of the southern escarpment of the Forest. The heaviest embankment was at the Marlborough end of the tunnel—although short, it contained 50,000 cu. yd and was 30 ft high. Some of the surplus chalk was deposited at Marlborough station, giving room for extra siding accommodation.

Fourteen bridges were built on the new railway and two reconstructed on the widened line south of Wolfhall. Hugh H. McClure designed them, the principal ones being the canal bridge at Savernake, 78 ft 5 in. long; the Great Bedwyn-Wolfhall road bridge, 68 ft 2 in.; and the 74 ft girder bridge over the GWR. The steelwork was made by Messrs Keay of Darlaston Works, Birmingham. All had steel plate girders, steel trough flooring and concrete abutments faced with brick.

At the board meeting of 29 April 1897, J. R. Shopland's death was reported; it was agreed that the balance of £350 of his salary, by this time £750, would be paid in monthly instalments of £25 to the representatives of his estate, on condition that they at their own cost did all the necessary work of carrying out the contract of Lucas & Aird. St George Moore was appointed engineer at a fee of 100 guineas and designed Savernake station.

The line from Marlborough to Wolfhall was inspected and passed by the Board of Trade on 15 June 1898.[8] The MGR had been built within two years of the passing of the Act.

> During the whole of Saturday night (June 25) gangs of men were busily engaged in making the connections between the new and the old lines at Marlborough and Wolfhall and the work was finished in time to enable the 7.52 a.m. passenger train out of Swindon to pass over the new course, the inauguration of which was signalised in railway fashion by a salute of fog signals.[9]

On this day, 26 June, the MSW junctions with the GWR at Marlborough and Savernake (Wolfhall Junction) were closed. The existing trains used the MGR and an improved service was run from 1 July 1898 when the MSW took over as tenants. It was a brilliant summer's day for the official opening ceremony on 2 July. Luncheon was served in the goods shed at Marlborough, which had been decorated with flags.

The MGR was absorbed on 1 August 1899 by the MSW Act of the same date.[10] The MSW was liable to pay a rent of £450 annually to the Marquess of Ailesbury for running over his land. The MGR board was finally dissolved on 11 January 1900. The MGR had raised £124,000 in share and loan capital and handed a balance of £9,602 14s 6d to the MSW. Sam Fay described the MGR as the keystone of the MSW's liberty.

The MSW Act 1899, section 8, mentioned the agreement made with the Marquess of Ailesbury[11] and the MGR was required 'to make and maintain a station adjacent to and at least equal to the existing station of the Great Western Railway Company at Savernake and to stop trains at such station under the provisions of the said agreement'.

IMPROVEMENTS TO EXISTING LINE

The *Railway Times* had said in January 1899 that the Midland Railway was trying to take over the MSW.

The prospect of a trunk line from the Midlands to Southampton may not be in immediate view, for no one who has seen the Midland & South Western Junction Railway would say that, at present, its track or equipment is of main-line standards. At the same time, through communication is a necessary step for such an outcome. . . *En passant*, it is worth noting that the traffic increase of over £4,000 in the past half year is far and away the largest proportional rise of any railway in the country. This is due almost entirely to the fact of the line running through the new army manoeuvre area in Wiltshire.

The growth of 1,000 in the number of first-class passengers and 54,000 in the third, shows a remarkable coincidence with the number of officers and men respectively—at two journeys each—known to have used this company's line on arriving for and leaving the manoeuvres. This is a source of revenue which must steadily increase, and that to a very large extent. For 1899 a scheme of divisional drilling on a very large scale extending over three months has already been announced. The projected establishment of a standing camp for 10,000 men will lead to an expansion in civilian as well as military traffic.[12]

The *Railway Times*[13] explained that an agreement[14] between the Midland Railway and the Midland & South Western had just been scheduled to the Midland Railway Company's bill then before Parliament. As the two systems were connected at Cheltenham by means of running powers over the GWR between Andoversford and Cheltenham, the two companies were agreeing to

give to each other every reasonable facility for the convenient working
and development of through traffic at rates and fares to be settled by
agreement or arbitration. With regard to through traffic between places
on the Midland Railway which are both south and west of Derby and
the following places on the London & South Western Railway—namely,
Andover, Southampton and Portsmouth, Lymington and places intermediate between Southampton and Lymington, including traffic reaching or leaving any of these places by water—the Midland Company
will so far as they lawfully can, cause such traffic to be carried over
the Junction Railway between Andover and Andoversford in preference
to any alternative route.

In return the MSW undertook to route as much traffic as possible
over the MR. The MR was to have running powers from Cheltenham
to Andoversford and to Southampton with the consent of the LSW,
in addition to running powers over the MSW. It was to retain 33⅓
per cent for working expenses, and the rest would go to the MSW
to provide increased accommodation for the through traffic. The
Midland offered to lend up to £50,000 each year for up to four years
at 3½ per cent. This money was used for doubling some of the
single-line sections and in 1902 a supplementary agreement lent
another £50,000.

Early in 1899, Fay negotiated with the GWR to double its Lansdown Junction to Andoversford Junction line within eighteen
months, and to undertake to provide within six months extra block
posts from Andoversford to Notgrove and Lansdown to Church-
down at places to be named by the MSW. The MSW was to be given
the right to stop for traffic at stations on the Banbury & Cheltenham
line between Cheltenham and Andoversford without extra payment.
This agreement was signed on 14 March 1899 and in return the
MSW withdrew a scheme for an extension northward to Ashchurch.

This was the last thing Fay did for the company, as he resigned
as from 15 April, returning to the LSW as superintendent. James
Purkess was his successor as general manager (see section on staff at
the end of this chapter), and E. T. Lawrence took over the
secretaryship.

The MSW gave notice to the GWR that doubling of the Cirencester
to Andoversford section would be completed by 1 November 1901.[15]
Messrs Firbank agreed to carry out the contract for £46,500. The
southern section was also doubled[16] and the tablet instruments at
Weyhill, Ludgershall and Collingbourne stations bought for £10
each from Messrs Saunders, so that in time of emergency single-line
working could be easily adopted and the use of pilotmen avoided.
Weyhill to Ludgershall and Andoversford to Withington were

inspected after doubling by Major Pringle on 24 August 1900 and opened to traffic on 28 August and 2 September respectively. He also inspected a new block post put in at Cerney, designed to assist punctuality on the Cirencester-Swindon section which was to remain single. The double line between Ludgershall and Collingbourne was opened on 1 September 1901 and that between Cirencester and Foss Cross on 12 July 1901.

Collingbourne to Grafton was opened as a double line on 2 November 1902, completing the 17¾ miles of double line between Weyhill and Marlborough. The double line between Foss Cross and Withington was inspected and passed on 3 June 1902 and opened to traffic on the 8th, Chedworth becoming a block post. (The same month, residents sent a petition for a siding to be put in at Chedworth, but the general manager replied that it was impracticable to provide one.) The line north of Cirencester was now double throughout and on 28 September the GWR doubling from Andoversford to Lansdown Junction, Cheltenham, was also completed.

A bay line and platform at Ludgershall, and an engine shed and turntable at a cost of £4,400, were provided at the War Department's expense.[17] At the end of the South African war, the Under-Secretary for War sent a letter thanking the company for carrying personnel, horses and stores *en route* for South Africa. Less happily, in 1905 Rushey Platt station needed rebuilding and receipts from passenger traffic were so small that the expense would not be warranted; the station was closed to passengers on 1 October.

Meanwhile Wolfhall junction with a loop siding between the Kennet & Avon canal bridge and the GWR south box was reopened for wagon transfers on 1 November 1900. The minutes in October 1901 said that on completion of the junction works the GWR would reduce the MSW's payment in respect of the signal box and junction at the Great Western end of Wolfhall from £180 to £52. The new junction and signal box at the Grafton end cost £1,100 and this was borne by the MSW. The maintenance charges of Wolfhall siding were to be paid by the MSW, but the Great Western paid half of the initial cost of £1,000.

Because of the increase of military traffic during the South African war, the former trailing connection was replaced by a facing connection worked from a new signal box—Wolfhall Junction (MSW).[18] The single-line spur between the MSW and GW box was worked by an electric train staff. The cost of £1,010 for this staff was shared between the two railways, but the MSW maintained it. Grafton curve was authorised by the GWR Act of 15 August 1904 and Wolfhall Junction (MSW) box was moved to a spot further south away from the canal bridge (see Chapter 8).

To facilitate working between each other's systems, it was agreed on 30 October 1901 that GWR engines should run over the line from Wolfhall junction to Ludgershall and MSW engines to Devizes or Westbury (neither company had engines shedded at Savernake).

Military traffic further increased with the opening of the Ludgershall-Tidworth branch: see next chapter.

1914-18 WAR

The company's best year financially proved to be 1913 but even so could not be described as successful. Just over £25,000 was available for distribution, or less than 1¼ per cent on the whole of the capital. The sum was sufficient to pay the 3 per cent interest on the top-ranking stocks, ½ per cent on 'B' debentures and over £5,000 of the MR loan, but left nothing for the 'C' debenture holders and the lower categories.

The first world war made an immediate impact. As early as the beginning of August 1914, guards as well as footplate crews were needed to act as pilotmen to Great Western drivers travelling from Grafton curve to Ludgershall or Tidworth taking troops to manoeuvres. Twenty-eight trains were involved, taking the London Brigade to their summer camp. With the announcement of the outbreak of war, the twenty-seventh train was stopped at Newbury and the twenty-eighth at Reading and the other twenty-six reloaded and returned.

Many MSW men wanted to join up, but John Davies, general manager, thought they would help their country more in their normal jobs; Davies persuaded the recruiting officers in the district not to accept MSW men unless they could produce a chit signed personally by him. One MSW man who wanted to enlist was prevented from doing so at Andover and Marlborough and had to go outside MSW territory to Devizes before he was accepted.

The MSW not only served military camps but also carried war supplies from the north to the Channel ports, while endless streams of hospital trains ran from Southampton to the north. Old people still say 'Them trains never stopped'. Regular runs were made with wounded from Dieppe and Cherbourg, the men still plastered with Flanders mud. Extra trains took casualties from the Gallipoli campaign in August 1915. Drivers were sometimes so busy working the ambulance trains that they did not see their families for a

COPYABLE.

REPEATED LETTER.—IMMEDIATE.

Midland & South Western Junction Railway.

Refer hereto in
your Reply.

GENERAL MANAGER'S THROUGH TRAFFIC OFFICE,
Cirencester, Glos.

Your

88/1132 48

(158)

Jan. 19ᵗʰ 1905.

DEAR SIR,

G W wagon 94064 Aug 30ᵗʰ to Sep. 3ʳᵈ

1 day 3/-

I shall feel obliged by your immediate reply to
my letter of the 16/12/04

respecting the above subject.

Yours truly,

J. PURKESS.

Mr Astley
Rushey Platt

fortnight at a time, occasionally working twenty-four hours without a rest.

The first ambulance trains were allotted only one engine and sometimes stalled between Foss Cross and Chedworth. On one occasion, a doctor told the guard that the efforts of the driver to get the engine up had thrown seven men off their stretchers. Later two engines were used—the LSW engine, usually a 4—4—0, was left on and an MSW engine put in front as pilot. The stock for the ambulance trains was provided by the larger companies. People who lived beside the line at Swindon Town and other places would hand jugs of tea to the troops on the trains. As well as through troop trains, trains ran to carry men between Tidworth and Southampton Docks. In 1918 when the submarine menace was severe, some of the American troops brought to Liverpool and Glasgow were taken to Southampton by the MSW. The locomotive foreman at Cheltenham would superintend the putting on of an MR 0—6—0 as pilot engine to assist up the incline to Andoversford Junction as it was against the MSW's principles to use bankers. On one occasion when the 0—6—0 had not returned from assisting the previous train, the troop-train driver started off on his own and stalled between Leckhampton and Charlton Kings. Fortunately an MSW goods train was following on behind and with its help the troops moved on. Stuart P. Johnstone made notes of some of the engines and coaches on troop trains:

1918	Description	Loco	Coaches
July 10	American troop	MR 509 (4—4—0)	Caledonian
12	Ambulance from S'ton	LSW 299 (4—4—0) &	10 GCR
		MSW No. 9	(8-wheel bogies)
15	American troop	MR 493 (4—4—0) &	SCE
		3678 (0—6—0)	
16	American troop empty stock from S'ton	MR 499 (4—4—0)	
16	,,	MR 497 (4—4—0)	
19	,,	MR 504 (4—4—0) &	
		77 (2—4—0)	
19	American troops to S'ton	MR 493 (4—4—0) &	
		3678 (0—6—0)	
Nov 9	,,	MR 493 (4—4—0) &	17 CLC 6-wheel
		3689 (0—6—0)	coaches + one 12-wheel bogie
1919			
Feb 11	Demobilised soldiers	MSW 23	17 LNW small 6-wheel coaches

At the beginning of the war an outside-cylinder MR goods engine was borrowed, but its power proved too weak for the banks and it was returned. Small hoppers were lent by the LSW, one at a time. No. 384 was the first; it had cross tubes in the firebox and was less efficient than Nos. 442 and 139, lent subsequently, which were free running. In 1916, in addition to running Red Cross trains over the line, an Adams 4—4—0 regularly worked an up afternoon train from Andover, returning with the 5.15 p.m. from Cheltenham. 4—4—0s Nos. 135 and 723 were also on loan, as was an Adams 0—4—2 tank engine. An Adams 4—4—2 radial tank engine worked between Andover, Ludgershall and Tidworth.

In November 1914 the GWR lent 0—6—0 tank engines Nos. 1036, 1228, 1264 and 1620, and Dean goods Nos. 2409 and 2429. Dean goods No. 2308 and 'Bulldog' Nos. 3310, 3320, 3441 and 0—6—0T No. 2799 also worked on the MSW, and GWR No. 2390 was stationed at Swindon Town. In 1916, No. 1036 was working on the Tidworth branch. Engines belonging to four companies were stationed at Ludgershall at this time (GWR, MR, LSW and MSW), shared among five sets of men. On one occasion the sidings at Ludgershall held coaches from the Highland Railway, North British Railway, LNW, MR, GCR, GWR, LSW and NER; on another occasion, after a breakdown at the northern end of the line, one of the regular passenger trains, instead of consisting of MSW stock, was made up of ancient LNW six-wheel coaches drawn by a GWR 0—6—0 saddle-tank. In 1917 some through trains were worked by Midland Railway 0—6—0s Nos. 3155, 3219 and 3464 and 4—4—0s Nos. 490 and 509. GWR 4—4—0 No. 3545 was on loan to the MSW in 1919, remaining until August 1920.

During the war the MSW carried the staggering totals of 181,683 officers and 2,992,202 men; it ran 6,452 specials in addition to 1,488 ambulance trains; it carried 134,852 horses, nearly 8,000 guns, 5,730 cycles, 15,176 tons of baggage and 9,021 ammunition trucks. The 1916 engine mileage was 1,118,255.[19]

On 28 September 1916 the secretary reported that

in order to facilitate the working of military traffic between Weyhill and Andover Junction and avoid the heavy delays that are now taking place, it had been proposed to construct a loop and junction between the Midland & South Western Junction Railway and the main line of the London & South Western Railway at Red Post which would give the necessary accommodation to enable the increased traffic passing to and from our line at Andover Junction to be more expeditiously and economically dealt with.

The War Office was requested to pay the cost of £5,131, and sell back the junction at a reasonable price at the end of the Government control of railways, the price to be shared between the two companies. The new junction was opened in 1917.

An agreement was made with the LSW on 1 June 1917 for additional works at Red Post, and on 5 January 1919 Red Post Junction was brought into use—an LSW signal box (1m 660 yd west of Andover Junction West box), a new MSW up loop, and junctions between both MSW loops and the up and down LSW main lines. A Tyer's No. 6 electric train tablet was installed for the single-line section Andover West-Red Post Junction and MSW tablet thence to Weyhill.

After the war a platform was provided at Chiseldon Camp, the Southern Command demobilisation centre.

POST-WAR YEARS AND GWR ABSORPTION

In 1921 the MSW staff applied for and received a rise in salaries and the railway's other expenses also increased. On 27 October 1921 it was proposed and carried by the board that

> in view of the very serious position disclosed by the returns, showing as compared with the pre-war figures increases in expenses out of all proportion to the increase in earning, the General Manager is instructed to use his utmost efforts to economize in every possible direction and especially to postpone all repairs, renewals and improvements not absolutely required in the interests of safety.

Early in 1923 a plan was discussed for doubling the line between Cirencester and Swindon Town, with a connection at the GWR overbridge (GWR post 79¼) between Swindon and Purton on the Gloucester line. This would have allowed trains a direct run from Blunsdon to Swindon Junction and saved nine miles between Cheltenham St James and Swindon, but there was not sufficient potential traffic to justify the work.

The Railways Act of 19 August 1921 allowed the GWR to absorb the MSW. On 8 October 1921 the actual control of the MSW passed to the Gloucester and Bristol Great Western divisional superintendents, but the MSW staff were left intact, theoretically the company still being independent. On 3 November 1921, the GWR drawing office made a dossier[20] of MSW equipment in preparation for the final absorption which had to be approved by the Railways Amalgamation Tribunal. The date of absorption by the GWR was delayed by MSW debts: the company was hopelessly over-capitalised, with more than £2 million ranking for dividend, including a loan of £244,000 from the Midland Company on which interest of about

SMA LOCOMOTIVES

(17) SMA *No.* 1

(18) *No. 4 Fairlie's patent locomotive at Swindon Town*

BEYER PEACOCK LOCOMOTIVES

(19) SMA *No. 7*
(20) SMA *No. 10*
(21) MSW *No. 24*

£5,000 was paid annually. The priority stocks occasionally received a dividend, but the lower stocks nothing at all. At grouping the wretched preference and ordinary shareholders received only £4 and £2 respectively for each £100 share.

L. B. Carslake, the MSW solicitor, met the Great Western's solicitor in mid-May 1922 to discuss the MSW's debt to the Midland. The Great Western solicitor said the debt was not a liability the GWR was obliged to take over with amalgamation. The problem was settled in March 1923 when Carslake received a letter from Mears, the LMS solicitor, stating that he was prepared to advise his clients to accept half of the £170,280, say £85,000, of the 5 per cent preference stock the MSW would receive from the Great Western in discharge of the amount advanced to the MSW by the Midland Railway Company.

The actual date of absorption was 1 July 1923. On 9 August the shareholders held a meeting to grant £3,000 to the directors for loss of office. Finally on 28 September 1923 the GWR (M & SWJR) Absorption Scheme of the same date was approved. The legal control by the GWR was effective from 29 October 1923.

When absorbed by the GWR the MSW owned 60m 55ch of route mileage and worked 2m 33ch (the Tidworth Camp Railway). It also exercised running powers over 37m 22ch of other companies' lines:

29m 28ch LSW Red Post Jc-Southampton
6m 72ch GWR Andoversford Jc-Lansdown Jc
1m 2ch MR Lansdown Jc-Cheltenham High St

STAFF

Sam Fay was secretary and general manager only between 1892 and 1899 but his influence was profound. He had joined the London & South Western Railway when he was 15½, as junior clerk at Itchen Abbas station. Publication of some of his literary work brought him recognition by the LSW management and in 1884 he was moved to the traffic superintendent's office at Waterloo, and appointed chief clerk a few months later. In 1891 he became assistant storekeeper at Nine Elms, and when the MSW approached his company in its search for a vigorous manager, he was the man thought most suitable. When he left in 1899 to rejoin the LSW as superintendent, succeeding the late G. T. White, the MSW chairman and directors paid him no more than his due in expressing

the deep obligation which they personally and the whole body of Stock and Shareholders are under to him for the skill and energy with

E

which he had managed the affairs of the Company for the last seven years, whereby its future prosperity has been assured . . . they desire gratefully to recognize that this result is largely due to his foresight and skilful management of the affairs of the Company.

At one complimentary dinner held in Cheltenham, a speaker described him as having 'made an empty sack stand upright'.

Fay had also endeared himself to the men by introducing a non-contributory pension scheme which he announced on the lawn in front of the Swindon offices. Up to a guinea a week was given; the arrangement is still honoured. Fay himself often said that his seven years at Swindon were among the happiest of his life.

Fay later joined the Great Central Railway (on 1 January 1902), confident that he could make this almost bankrupt line a paying proposition as he had the MSW. He worked wonders with it, and King George V, opening Immingham Dock on the Humber on 22 July 1912, asked Fay to kneel and unexpectedly knighted him. In the first world war he became 'Director-General of Movements and Railways', and lived to be ninety-seven, dying on 30 May 1953.

Fay's successor as general manager of the MSW was James Purkess, who was appointed on 4 April 1899 at a salary of £500 a year plus 5 per cent of any increase of net revenue in any year over and above that for 1898. The salary with commission was guaranteed not to be below £1,000 a year and the agreement was to last for seven years. Purkess had started work as a junior clerk in that same storekeeper's office at Nine Elms, in 1873. When F. J. Macaulay was appointed the LSW's secretary, Purkess became his amanuensis, and in March 1892 he had a special appointment in the general manager's office, in due course becoming chief assistant to the general manager. Fay himself recommended him as his own successor with the MSW. During his regime receipts increased by 50 per cent—and considering that Fay had managed the line so ably this was no mean achievement. He saw that the railway's equipment was much augmented and had great attention paid to improving the stability of the permanent way.

He died suddenly. On 29 November 1902 he called at the Swindon office and complained to Lawrence, the secretary, that he was suffering from a cold and was going to his home, Queen's Hill House, Cirencester, to bed. He died on 11 December, the immediate cause being suppressed typhoid fever. He was only forty-three and left a widow and five children. He was buried at Long Ditton, Surbiton, on 16 December, and a special train carried the coffin and the mourners from Cirencester to Surbiton. As a tribute, the foot-

Midland & South Western Junction Rly.

CHEAP EXCURSIONS

TO

MARLBOROUGH

FOR

SAVERNAKE FOREST

(By kind permission of Lord Ailesbury).

On August 2nd, 3rd, 4th, 6th, 7th, 8th, 9th, 10th & 11th.

CHEAP TICKETS WILL BE ISSUED TO

MARLBOROUGH

AS UNDER :—

LUGERSHALL dep. 12.12 & 5.17 p.m.

Return Fare { First Class **2/-**
Third Class **1/-**

Passengers Return from MARLBOROUGH 4.36, 6.53 & 9.10 p.m.

From a tourist's point of view, the chief attraction at Marlborough is Savernake Forest, the only forest in the country belonging to a subject. It is 16 miles in circumference, and about 4,000 acres in area. The "Grand Avenue" of beech trees, planted in 1723, is five miles long, and the following quotation, descriptive of its beauties, will be recognised by all who have explored its recesses :—" Far as the eye can see extends an avenue of beech passing right through the forest. The tall smooth trunks rise up to a great height, and then branch overhead, looking like the roof of a Gothic cathedral. The growth is so regular and so perfect that the comparison springs unbidden to the lips, and here, if anywhere, that order of architecture might have taken its inspiration. There is a continuous Gothic arch of green for miles, beneath which one may drive or walk as in the aisles of a forest abbey." The forest abounds with fine old oaks, the principal being known as the "King Oak" (24 feet in circumference), "The Duke's Vaunt," the "Queen Oak," and "Braydon Oak."

CHILDREN UNDER 12, HALF-PRICE.

The Tickets are available on the day of issue only, by the Trains specified, and are not transferable ; if used otherwise the Full Ordinary Fares will be charged.

Swindon, August, 1906. **JOHN DAVIES, General Manager.**

"North Wilts Herald" Offices, Bath Road & Faringdon Street, Swindon.

An excursion handbill of 1906

platemen at Cirencester did not start work until 10 a.m. and stopped work between 1 and 3 o'clock, the time of the funeral. That day, the *London Express* revealed that Purkess had been poisoned by eating oysters at the mayoral banquet he attended at Southampton on 10 November. Around the same date several other people had also died from eating polluted oysters from the south coast.

The new manager was John Davies, from the Midland Railway, who remained with the MSW from 31 December 1902 until the amalgamation. His salary on appointment was £750 a year, plus a commission of 5 per cent of any increase of revenue over that of 1902.

Davies had been for three years the general manager of the Central Wales & Carmarthen Junction Railway, which became part of the LNW. He was then offered the post of general manager of the Western Australian Government Railways, where he stayed eleven years, during which time mileage increased from 200 to 1,400 and annual revenue from £60,000 to £1,500,000. His work there was so much valued that on his departure he was given six months' leave on full pay and an honorarium of £1,000. The MSW must have felt itself to be again in good hands. After absorption in 1923 Davies retired to Cheltenham, dying there in April 1925.

When Fay departed, the secretaryship again became a separate office, held by E. T. Lawrence from 1899 to 1908. His salary on appointment was £150 a year plus commission. Lawrence left in 1908 to become secretary to the Barry Railway, and was replaced by S. H. Webber, who held the post until it was again combined with the general managership, under Davies, in 1917; Davies of course remained secretary until the amalgamation.

Eben Connal, a Scot with an immense sense of humour, who had been appointed resident engineer in charge of doubling the line in 1899, became engineer on 1 January 1903, at an annual salary of £400.[21] He remained here until the amalgamation, when he retired. Also in 1903, James Tyrrell was appointed locomotive and carriage superintendent. He had joined the SMA when the Cirencester-Andoversford line was opened in 1881, at the request of L. T. Haydon, the first head of the locomotive department, having first worked for the GWR. Tyrrell retired on grouping, but did not die until 1948, at the age of ninety-four.

J. M. Malerbi was another of the particularly energetic characters the MSW seemed to attract. He had been a clerk on the Mid-Wales Railway and stationmaster at Builth on that line. In 1900 he became the MSW district traffic superintendent at Southampton and did an excellent job of work, successfully canvassing for traffic. On 1 January 1924 he was transferred to the staff of the Great Western's Southampton agent and retired on 31 December 1925.

The traffic department employed 152 staff, Swindon having the most—twenty-three on passenger duties and fifteen on goods. Ludgershall and Tidworth came next, each employing sixteen. The locomotive department had 176 staff, fifty-four of them at the Cheltenham shed, eighteen at Andover shed and sixteen at Swindon. Details are shown in the table overleaf.

Porters wore a uniform of green corduroy trousers, sleeve waistcoat, jacket and pillbox hat. Footplatemen at one time had to provide their own clothes, and legend has it that one driver liked to wear white corduroys, and if his knees were dirty after he had knelt on the footplate, the cleaner would suffer. The cleaners had to scour the footwalks white as well as see to the handrails and smokebox-door hinges; they also had to coal the engine they were allotted. Drivers would sometimes leave 6d on the axleboxes so that the cleaner would find it if he did his job properly; some drivers would give their cleaner a packet of cigarettes at the end of the week for giving the engine an extra polish.

As an indication of wage rates, from 1 January 1914 gangers' pay was increased to 4s 4d per day for those at Cirencester, Swindon, Ludgershall and Tidworth stations, with 3s 10d per day for those elsewhere. Second men in all gangs were to have 3s 4d per day, and packers of over two years' service 3s 2d.

The company chair was occupied in turn by two Marquesses of Ailesbury, E. W. Cripps of Cirencester, F. C. Scotter (son of Sir Charles Scotter, former general manager and chairman of the LSW), and finally by S. J. Portal (son of another former chairman of the LSW). There were nine directors on the board, representing debenture holders (five), preference holders (two) and ordinary shareholders (two). Prominent members included Lord Bathurst, Sir William Acworth (author of *The Railways of England*), A. L. Goddard of Swindon and W. E. Nicolson Browne of Chiseldon.

MSW EMPLOYEES 19 March 1921
—From Ministry of Transport Statistics

	Adults	Juniors under 18
LOCO DEPT		
Engine drivers	32	—
Firemen	32	—
Engine cleaners	20	8
CARRIAGE & WAGON DEPT		
Carriage cleaners	7	—
Carriage and wagon examiners	5	—
Carriage and wagon oilers and greasers	2	—
Labourers	13	—
MECHANICS & ARTISANS	91	4
ALL DEPTS		
Clerks (male)	87	3
„ (female)	1	—
Inspectors	7	—
Cranemen	2	1
Miscellaneous (male)	32	2
„ (female)	1	—

CHAPTER 5

Branch Lines

Toward the end of the nineteenth century there was a spate of schemes for extending the line at the northern end, avoiding having to use the steeply-graded GWR between Andoversford and Chelten- ham. The Stroud Valley, Honeybourne, Stratford on Avon and Ashchurch were among the targets. Of these, the Ashchurch line came the nearest to being built and under an agreement of 14 March 1899, in return for the scheme being dropped, the GWR conceded the right of the MSW to fix its own rates over the Andoversford- Cheltenham section as though it were its own route. The section concerned was also doubled by the GWR as a result of this agree- ment, and the Midland Railway too was granted running powers over it.

Another project which interested many people was that for link- ing the MSW with the little East Gloucestershire Railway at Witney or Fairford; this would have provided a more direct route from Cheltenham to London, through Oxford, incidentally one of the first through routes where the traffic later suffered from road competition. As early as 1897 there was an experimental road-rail service in connection with the MSW at Cirencester's Watermoor station. The road vehicle, which ran to Fairford, was a solid-tyre, oil-burning, steam-driven motor van carrying 2½-3 tons of parcels, drawing a twenty-seater passenger trailer. Sometimes the passengers had to transfer to the main vehicle to give it extra adhesion on hills.

As has already been told, in the early days there were plans for an extension southward to the Solent. There were also plans to give the MSW conventional feeder branches. One such was for a branch from Marlborough to Calne and Hungerford. Another ran from Collingbourne through a line of villages in the Avon valley to Fittleton, while there was once talk of a line from Ludgershall to Amesbury military camp. In the event, only the Tidworth branch was ever built.

THE TIDWORTH BRANCH

One of the first things James Purkess did on becoming general manager was to seek an interview with the War Department about building a railway between Ludgershall and the new military camp being established at Tidworth. The line was built under an agreement of 19 November 1900 between the MSW and War Office, and constructed on the latter's land. It cost £47,905 11s 9d, and was opened for military manoeuvre traffic on 8 July 1901.

A few months earlier, in January, the War Department had been asked to allow the branch to be a public railway. This resulted in an agreement dated 22 October 1901 for the temporary working and maintenance of the Ludgershall & Tidworth railway. The MSW was to be paid its expenditure plus 10 per cent of the profit, and in return would only carry (in addition to War Office materials) the traffic of such traders as the WD approved. The line was opened for War Department goods traffic on 21 May 1902 and public traffic on 1 July, and to public passengers on 1 October 1902. It was staffed and worked by the MSW under a further agreement of 16 February 1903, when it was leased to the MSW for fourteen years at a rental of 3 per cent on a capital expenditure of £47,905 11s 9d, equal to £1,437 3s 6d per annum[1], the MSW maintaining the line and taking receipts, including 2s 6d for every wagon worked over it. The line was double to Perham box, half a mile from Ludgershall, but the box was usually switched out and line worked single throughout. There was a rise of 1 in 85 to the summit and a descent of 1 in 90 to Tidworth's station on the Hampshire-Wiltshire border.

In 1902 a Mr Lovatt wanted to put in a siding on the line at Brimstone Bottom. This was formally agreed on 27 April 1903 and he was allowed to convey his workmen between the village of Brimstone Bottom and Tidworth by his own engines, vehicles and staff, for a yearly toll.

The MSW's lease was extended at 5 per cent for a further fourteen years in 1917 and again in 1931. On nationalisation it was leased by the War Office to the British Transport Commission. The public passenger service was withdrawn on 19 September 1955, the working agreement terminating on 24 November and all traffic being handled by the War Department itself after 28 November. Closure came on 31 July 1963, but the line to the Central Vehicle Depot is still open and worked by two Army Ruston & Hornsby diesel locomotives.

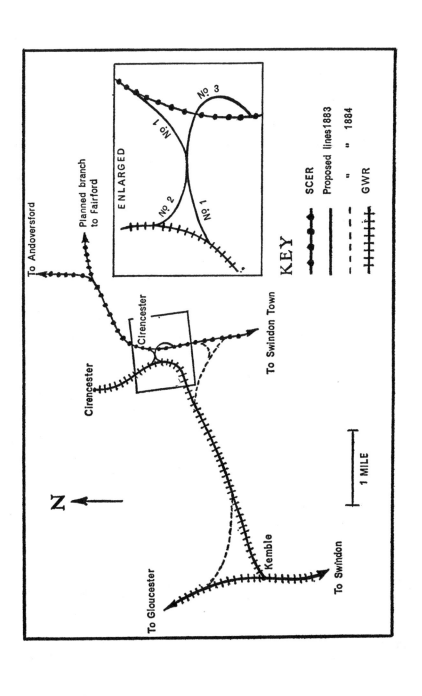

To Andoversford

Planned branch to Fairford

Cirencester

Cirencester

Cirencester

To Swindon Town

To Gloucester

Kemble

To Swindon

N

1 MILE

ENLARGED

Nº 3

Nº 1

Nº 2

Nº 1

KEY

SCER

Proposed lines 1883

" " 1884

GWR

The branch well justified its existence. In 1922, for instance, the garrison could accommodate five infantry and three cavalry battalions—about 8,000 men—while up to 100,000 were accommodated in summer camps in surrounding districts. Tidworth's two long platforms, the longer reserved for military traffic, its central road, extensive goods sidings and other facilities were frequently pressed into service. The seven roads in the yard held 290 wagons, or ten trains of twelve coaches each. One track was known as the 'meat road'; a twenty-eight-wagon meat train arrived weekly during the first world war. Beyond the station the War Office had about 2½ miles of its own lines and sidings, and kept its own stud of locomotives. About 1930, No. 2196 *Gwendreath* of the former Burry & Gwendreath Valley Railway was lent by the GWR for shunting duties at the barracks. The camp system closed in 1953.[2]

But quite apart from the barracks traffic, the Tidworth branch had a busy career, and receipts at Tidworth (the only MSW station lit by electricity) were the greatest on the system, while the station was in charge of the railway's highest-ranking stationmaster. But undoubtedly the branch's highlights were the days of the Tidworth Tattoo, when trains came in from the GWR, SR and LMS and had to be stabled very carefully to enable them to leave in the right order. In the early days, incidentally, the branch was served by a four-coach set of six-wheelers, and later a three-coach articulated set which survived into GWR days.

THE DODSDOWN BRICKWORKS BRANCH
(contributed by D. J. Hyde)

The Army required large quantities of bricks to develop Salisbury Plain as a military training ground with depots at places such as Tidworth, Bulford and Larkhill. Clay suitable for brickmaking was not common in Wiltshire, and building materials were brought from all over the country for the vast barracks at Tidworth. In 1902 clay was found eight miles from Tidworth, at Dodsdown, near Wilton —two miles north-east of Grafton station. The land there was leased by the Marquess of Ailesbury to A. J. Keeble of Peterborough for £50 a year. He built a two-mile-long standard-gauge line from the small brickworks to a junction with the MSW on the two goods refuge sidings north of Grafton station. Bricks were conveyed to Grafton in open wagons, collected by MSW goods trains every day and taken to Tidworth and elsewhere. Coal for the kilns at the works was delivered to the Grafton sidings and taken with the returned empty brick wagons to Dodsdown.

At Grafton the sidings were on the east side of the main line, extending from the bridge over the Burbage to Hungerford road, into the cutting towards Grafton South Junction for about 300 yd. A crossover at the northern end made the two lines into a run-round loop, with a headshunt at the station end. The branch curved away eastwards from the sidings and dropped steeply for ¾ mile at approximately 1 in 90 as far as a small level crossing on the road from Grafton to Crofton and Bedwyn. Then came the only level stretch for ¼ mile, and the opportunity to run at a gradient of about 1 in 60, with a slight curve eastwards to avoid a natural lake known as Wilton Wide Water. The water was crossed at its southern end by a small three-arch brick-built bridge with the permanent way supported on 1 ft square timbers, and then climbed steeply to the north of Wilton village, running for ¼ mile to Dodsdown. The layout at Dodsdown was simple, consisting of three sidings serving dryers, kilns, boiler house and engine shed.

The locomotive used for the construction of the line and the first services was *A. J. Keeble*, an 0—6—0 outside-cylinder saddle tank, built by Peckett & Sons of Bristol in 1902, works No. 939. But when regular working began it was found that this locomotive could not always cope with the six-wagon trains. The practice was to propel the wagons from Grafton to Dodsdown and pull the load back to Grafton where the gradient was less, an important safety pre-caution in days when wagon couplings were of inferior steel. On several occasions, particularly in wet weather, the 0—6—0ST lost its grip and the complete train slid back down the gradient to the level crossing.

In 1907 *A. J. Keeble* went to the Wissington Light Railway, Norfolk, and was replaced by an 0—4—0 outside-cylinder saddle tank, also newly built by Peckett & Sons, with works No. 1080. It was named *Progress*. Braking was by handbrake only, surprising after the experience with the early engine and hazardous on those gradients. The first engine was painted a Midland lake and black with a brass dome, while *Progress* had a livery of apple green. They were owned by Keeble and officially were used exclusively on the private line, but apparently the staff at Grafton station were not above coming to terms with the driver of *Progress* when a van or two needed moving in Grafton yard on the south side of the station.

To keep the builders supplied and the brickworks provided with materials, trains ran as necessary, usually two journeys in each direction daily. They normally consisted of six wagons, four empty brick wagons and two loaded coal wagons from Grafton to Dodsdown, and four loaded brick and two empty coal wagons from Dodsdown to Grafton. The arrangement was suited both to the gradients up and down and to shunting at each end of the line. Driver and fireman were both local men.

The fireman had to open the gates at Heath Lane level crossing and of course close them after the train had passed; the width of the railway track bed was less than that of the road, so the gates were fitted with hinged extensions which had to be opened out when the gates were across the road. Local boys, knowing when a train was due, would sometimes have the gates already open, and after closing them would get their reward—a ride, either on the footplate or on the bricks, to Grafton station. On one occasion the driver had released his handbrake a little early on leaving Wilton and the train came down the 1 in 60 gradient without any hope of stopping at the level crossing—but the lads were there, the gates open, and *Progress* sped ½ mile further on to Grafton station before it could be stopped. The local lads would also gather bracken and long grass to clean out the brick dust and straw from the wagons.

Another incident which happily did not end in disaster occurred when, while shunting at Dodsdown, two wagons did not have their brakes properly pinned and ran down the gradient through the nine level-crossing gates[3], which this time were shut, and stopped just beyond on the level. This, of course, put the wagons on the 'wrong' side of the engine, which pulled them back to Dodsdown where the brickworks staff had to manhandle them back into the siding.

The barracks were complete by 1910 and the line closed and dismantled shortly afterwards, to the great disappointment of the local people from villages nearby, who used to walk for miles to see 'their' railway. *Progress* was sent to Sanderson Bros & Newbould Ltd, Sheffield.

The track formation can still be seen in many places, particularly either side of the level crossing at Heath Lane. The arches of the bridge across Wilton Water remain to this day, although crumbling. One of the level-crossing gateposts also remains as a memorial.

Chapter 6

Lines Associated with the MSW

THE ANDOVER & REDBRIDGE RAILWAY

Although much has inevitably been said already about the other railways which enabled the MSW to fulfil the role of a through route, it might be helpful to summarise the details of the dealings with them in a separate chapter. The MSW of course did not reach either Southampton in the south or Cheltenham in the north on its own rails, and during its early years even had to use the Marlborough Railway to link its two then unconnected sections.

The Andover & Redbridge Railway was especially vital to the MSW, unlocking as it did the door to Southampton. The first line with this title was under the auspices of the London & South Western Railway and was authorised in 1847 to purchase the almost derelict Andover & Redbridge Canal[1] and convert it into a railway[2], giving running powers to the Manchester & Southampton Railway. It was decided that the Andover to Southampton section would be jointly owned with the MSR, and in 1850 the LSW and the MSR put down £9,000 as deposit for the canal, this being distributed to the canal shareholders.[3] But owing to the financial difficulties following the Railway Mania, the powers lapsed.

In 1858, an independent railway with the same title, the Andover & Redbridge Railway, obtained powers to convert the canal into a broad-gauge railway to connect with a fourteen-mile line the Great Western proposed building from the Berks & Hants Extension Railway at Pewsey to Andover. After crossing the LSW at Redbridge, it was suggested continuing to an independent terminus at Southampton. The narrow-gauge LSW resented this thrust into its territory and opposed it unsuccessfully; then it tried to get a clause put into the Act stating that the gauge should be standard. This failed also and so did the LSW's final throw, an attempt to have a mixed-gauge clause put in. The Act received Royal Assent on 12 July 1858.[4] The capital of the ARR was £120,000, with loans of £43,000.

On 28 September 1859 the first sod was cut by Lord Palmerston, just outside his residence at Broadlands, Romsey. An Act of 15 May 1860[5] allowed a deviation, and completion was fixed for 12 July 1863. In a further Act of 29 July 1862[6], the railway was authorised to cancel forfeited shares and to raise a new capital of £15,000 at 5 per cent preference, and £5,000 on mortgage. The time of completion was extended to 1 January 1864. Lack of capital had delayed the work and the Great Western tried unsuccessfully to buy the bankrupt[7] and still unfinished concern.

In 1862 the GWR and the LSW made a truce, agreeing that the line should be London & South Western territory. Powers were given the following year[8], which were backdated to 14 November 1862, and the Act also authorised a deviation so that the line could join the Eastleigh to Salisbury branch at Romsey to avoid the expense of building an additional station. At Andover, the LSW was given powers to extend its line from Andover Town to Andover Junction so that it could join the Basingstoke to Salisbury line. The LSW took up the debenture debt and other liabilities, securing to the shareholders an annuity equal to 3 per cent on the payments it had made.[9]

The single-track 'sprat and winkle' line was opened throughout on 6 March 1865. There were passing loops at the stations—Andover Town, Clatford, Fullerton (from where a branch to Hurstbourne was opened on 1 June 1885), Stockbridge, Horsebridge, Mottisfont, Romsey, Nursling, Redbridge, Millbrook and Southampton West. The curves were tortuous through following the canal and were necessary to avoid the expense of crossing the river Test too frequently. Gradients were easy except between Andover Junction and Andover Town, where the incline of 1 in 62-81 covered nearly the whole distance, one mile. The line was doubled and much of it realigned in 1885.

THE MARLBOROUGH RAILWAY

Some of the other early schemes to give Marlborough a railway, and also the later history of the line so far as it affected the MSW, of which for a time it virtually formed a part, have already been told. It remains to describe how the small concern was born and built.

Immediately after the promotion of the Berks & Hants from Hungerford to Devizes, local people, led by the Marquess of Ailesbury, seized the chance of building a broad-gauge branch from the BHE at Savernake to a field called Cherry Orchard at Marlborough; in fact, the BHE Act had even gone so far as to suggest that a branch to Marlborough would be a good thing. Few difficulties presented themselves, as apart from 200 yd belonging to Marlborough College, all the land on which the line was to be built was owned by the Marquess. In December 1860, the Great Western promised to work the proposed line. The company's Act received Royal Assent on 22 July 1861.[10] It authorised a capital of £45,000, of which the GWR could have subscribed £20,000, though in fact it subscribed only half this amount.

After advertising the contract, John Knight's tender for the works, excluding stations, was accepted. Out of a total of £38,000, £15,000 was to be paid in ordinary shares and the balance in cash. He began work in January 1863 and by 23 March 15,000 cu. yd out of a total of 220,000 had been moved. Two months later works were sufficiently advanced to advertise a contract for the station buildings. A third of the earthworks were completed by November. In his report in September, R. J. Ward, the line's engineer, said that the fences were fixed, 166,000 cu. yd of embankment had been built and all the bridges were complete or well advanced. The permanent way was laid at Savernake for seven-eighths of a mile and the junction with the main line had been completed and signalled. However, bad weather in the winter delayed the work and the first train did not arrive in Marlborough until 2 March 1864.

Captain F. H. Rich of the Board of Trade inspected the line on 8 March and found that the heavy embankment near Marlborough was not sufficiently firm to allow public opening. The faulty embankment was soon consolidated by heavy ballast trains, but re-inspection was delayed as Captain Yolland was ill and Captain Rich had extra work thrown on his shoulders. He passed the line after his visit on 30 March when he had quite an exciting time. The engine the Great Western supplied stalled many times on the gradients of 1 in 58-60, and rumour had it that passengers got out and pushed. This led to humorous postcards being sold in Marlborough with the train depicted as the Marlborough Donkey and the caption:

> You may push and you may shuv
> But I'm hanged if I'll be druv.

Captain Rich, in returning thanks for the toast at the post-inspection luncheon, said:

> If all present patronise it as they ought, I have no doubt that the dividends and everything else will be satisfactory. I hope you will

have something better for an engine to carry you, not to be stopped midway, but that was from no fault in the line. It was not the curves, nor the gradients, for I have inspected lines with much greater, but the incapacity of the engine, which was nothing more or less than an old ballast engine, not quite equal to the work.[11]

The Marquess of Ailesbury's comment that the line would appear in *Bradshaw* in a few days led a man to come from Avebury to travel on it and find to his chagrin that traffic would not begin until after the meeting with the Great Western Board. The Marlborough Railway was opened on 14 April 1864 and a horse bus connected it with Calne. In October the directors discussed extending the line as far as Calne, but decided against the idea.

Traffic during the first few years did not reach expectations and for the six months ending December 1866 only averaged £6 a mile weekly. By 1870 the financial position had improved and a dividend of 6 per cent was declared. In 1871 a Marlborough man, James Leader, was appointed secretary of the company; it was hoped that this would further encourage interest. During the first six months of 1872, 18,315 passengers and 7,160 tons of goods were carried.

The railway was converted to standard gauge on 27 June 1874, reopening on 1 July, the Berks & Hants Extension being altered at the same time. The GWR had told the Marlborough Railway that the estimated cost of the conversion would be £2,600 and that it would lend the money. The Marlborough Railway replied that it had no funds and its borrowing powers were completely taken up; even an interest of 5 per cent on the cost would render an ordinary dividend only an irregular occurrence. Later it was amicably arranged that the Marlborough Railway would pay half the cost, not exceeding £750, at 4 per cent. The Great Western accountants seem to have been pleasantly slow, not working out the expense of narrowing until 1877 and fortunately only charging the Marlborough line £296 11s 8d. All this was of course before MSW trains began using the line, as related earlier.

The Marlborough Railway was vested in the GWR in July 1896, £12 of Great Western stock being given for each share; preference shares and debentures were exchanged for GWR securities giving the same income.

THE BANBURY & CHELTENHAM DIRECT RAILWAY

A plan for the Cheltenham & Bourton-on-the-Water Railway was deposited on 30 November 1860[12], indicating roughly the same

MSW LOCOMOTIVES—1

(22) *No. 4 with double-domed boiler*
(23) *No. 6 at Eastleigh, April 1922*

MSW LOCOMOTIVES—2

(24) *No. 9 at Andover, with stovepipe chimney, c. 1899*
(25) *No. 9 at Cirencester, c. 1900, now with iron-capped chimney*

course as the later Banbury & Cheltenham Direct Railway adopted. The scheme was unsuccessful.

Three years later, a modified plan[13] sought a bill to authorise the Great Western to contribute £450,000 out of the £600,000 capital needed. The line was to be altered near Cheltenham: instead of making a junction with the GWR and MR, it was to leave the GWR nearer the terminus and pass under the built-up outskirts of the town in a tunnel 1,474 yd long. The owners of property near this proposed tunnel organised powerful opposition and the bill was defeated. In 1864 the MR was induced to promise £100,000 towards a similar scheme and agreed to work the line at 50 per cent of gross receipts, but the GWR attacked the MR under the 1863 agreement and prevented it making the promised subscription.[14]

The Banbury & Cheltenham Direct Railway plan was deposited 30 November 1872[15] and was for a railway from Bourton to a point near the 119¼ milepost just south of Cheltenham. A triangular junction was proposed at Cheltenham as in the first scheme. The BCD Act received Royal Assent on 21 July 1873, and authorised the GWR and the Bourton-on-the-Water Railway to arrange working agreements. On 10 November 1874, Edward Wilson, the engineer, was instructed to proceed with construction. Deviations were sought in 1875 and 1876 near Sandywell Park. Work on the line was suspended during the financial crisis of 1878 and not restarted until late in 1879.

The Cheltenham to Bourton-on-the-Water section was given priority as all the stations except one had been finished and twelve of the 16½ miles laid with permanent way. Difficulties were experienced with the clay between Cheltenham and Andoversford; when excavated it was almost as hard as stone, but on exposure to air and damp it slaked like lime. The line was single, but overline bridges as far as Andoversford and also the tunnel were built for a double track. The permanent way was of double-headed rail weighing 80 lb per yd.

Col F. H. Rich inspected the BCD in March 1881.[16] He found that Charlton Kings station was not marked in the original plans and required the curve to be eased; a wooden footbridge and staircase at the station required strengthening; the station platforms were too far from the rails—he said that the steps of the coaches should have been allowed to come within 2 in. of the edge; he recommended that clocks be provided at all the stations, and the platform fencing completed at Andoversford; heavy slips at the end of the tunnel had to be drained by cuttings and pipes. Col Rich would not, in fact,

F

allow the opening to passenger traffic, requiring two subsequent inspections before passing the line.

It finally opened on 1 June 1881. The first train was the 6.50 a.m. from Cheltenham, with eleven coaches and George Allen, a director, McIntyre the engineer, and R. B. Looker, the secretary. No great interest was shown in the new line and the *Cheltenham Free Press* gave the opinion that the line to Southampton would be more important. This paper was antagonistic to the MR, GWR and LNW and pointed out the possibilities of travelling to London (Waterloo) *via* Andover, a journey only twelve miles longer than the GWR route to Paddington *via* Swindon. The story of how MSW trains used the Cheltenham-Andoversford section, which was later doubled, has already been told.

CHAPTER 7

Decline and Death

GREAT WESTERN ECONOMIES

The MSW was the biggest subsidiary, as distinct from constituent, company to be absorbed as part of the Great Western. This, the last of the absorptions, was completed when the Railways Amalgamation Tribunal approved the scheme on 28 September 1923.[1] Territorially it was right that the MSW should have gone to the GWR, but it is interesting to speculate what would have happened if it had been made into a joint line like the Somerset & Dorset Railway and run by the LMS and SR.

The Great Western took over 29 locomotives, 134 coaches, 260 goods and 119 service vehicles. As absorption had been anticipated, provision had been made in the 1922 renumbering scheme. The engines were taken into GWR stock during the four weeks ending 1 December 1923.

The GWR was anxious to make economies and the MSW headquarters at Swindon was closed in 1924 and its staff dispersed to various offices and stations. Red Post to Rushey Platt was placed in the Bristol District and Rushey Platt to Andoversford in the Gloucester District. (The GWR's administrative staff often had little knowledge of the route, and for some years the Bristol District control frequently consulted the Tidworth stationmaster, the unofficial spokesman for the ex-MSW system.) The MSW was classified as a 'yellow' weight-restriction route, which meant that only a very limited selection of engines could travel over it. The locomotive, carriage and wagon works at Cirencester were closed in 1924, as described in Chapter 10. The MSW locomotive shed at Swindon was closed on 21 January 1924, and the engines stabled at Swindon Junction; the shed at Swindon Town became a bus garage and was later taken over by an oil company.

One of the minor changes under the new regime was that guards had to choose to work either passenger or goods trains; MSW guards had worked both. The MSW had also employed 'assistant guards' who did not, as the title implies, work under a guard, but had trains of their own; employees considered the measure a trick by the company to get away with paying them 2s a week less. Some of the MSW drivers had antipathies to the Great Western and on absorption moved to Eastleigh and joined the SR.

In July 1924 a single stationmaster became responsible for both stations at Marlborough and the same economy was made at Savernake a year later. A proposal was made for building a central signal box at Savernake which would also have worked the Grafton curves, but the estimated cost of £3,340 was thought to be too high. Another economy was made in October 1925 when the Tidworth goods agent retired and the depot was placed under the stationmaster. The old junction between the GWR and the MSW at Marlborough which had been removed in 1898 was reopened in 1926 (see Chapter 8).

Even with these economies, it was thought extravagant to keep two routes open between Savernake and Marlborough. As early as 1922 Paddington decided to remodel the Savernake-Marlborough service. Double-track junctions to the MSW line were to be put in between Wolfhall Junction MSW and Wolfhall Junction GW, and immediately west of the Great Western Savernake station at an estimated cost of £30,000. It was intended to lift the GWR Marlborough branch, saving £1,600 in annual maintenance costs and the wages of three signalmen. The scheme had the disadvantage of introducing a gradient of 1 in 60 at Wolfhall, whereas the steepest MSW gradient was 1 in 75, but W. W. Grierson, the GWR engineer, suggested that the existing MSW line should be retained for goods traffic.

The *North Wilts Herald*[2] announced that it had been definitely decided to close the line from Savernake Low Level to Marlborough High Level from 1 April 1929. An experimental service of modern buses seating thirty-two passengers was to replace the trains. Then on 28 March[3] it was announced that the branch would not be closed, as Paddington was reviewing the situation. The outcome was that the double track of the Marlborough & Grafton Railway from Marlborough through Savernake Tunnel and for some distance southwards was made into two single lines for independent use (see also Chapter 8). The former down line was to continue to serve Savernake High Level, while the erstwhile Marlborough Railway was diverted into the MGR up line at Hat Gate, where the two lines ran very close. The rest of the Marlborough Railway was abandoned except for a shunting neck at Marlborough. The shuttle service from

Savernake Low Level to Marlborough High Level was diverted into Marlborough Low Level station and the high-level station closed to passengers. These modifications came into use on 6 March 1933, and all trains, except two calling at Savernake High Level, were diverted to Savernake Low Level. The capital cost of the alteration was £13,436 and the length of the Great Western branch lifted 4m. 73½ch. (See map on page 52.)

At the same time, Grafton Curve (Berks & Hants Line) signal box was renamed Grafton East Junction signal box, and Wolfhall Junction (MSW Section) box renamed Grafton South Junction. The existing double-line blocks from Marlborough to Savernake High Level and Savernake High Level to Wolfhall Junction (MSW) were taken out of use and a new single-line block section made from Marlborough to Grafton South Junction, worked by an electric train token with a looped siding and intermediate token instrument at Savernake High Level. Savernake West signal box to Marlborough High Level electric staff was replaced by an electric train token and the up direction became the down to conform with the MSW section terminology. All trains from Savernake to Marlborough were then 'up'. Savernake High Level signal box became a two-lever ground frame known as Savernake Middle Ground Frame. 336 yd west of it was Savernake West Ground Frame and 246 yd east, Savernake East Ground Frame working the refuge siding (loop). Both ground frames were released by the token. All trains used the up platform, the down being left as a loop siding not available for passenger trains. On 15 February 1933 a new signal box was opened at Marlborough replacing the GWR and MSW boxes.

Wolfhall Junction exchange sidings had become redundant and the inner of the two was relaid as an additional running line, so that from the GWR Wolfhall Junction box to Grafton South the line was only single over the 90 ft long canal bridge. Track circuiting was installed and train movements over it controlled from the signal boxes at each end by special levers in each box, electrically interlocked so that they could not be pulled together. The electric staff could then be abolished between the two boxes; this was one of the first stretches in the country to have single-line working without staff or token.

The line from Cirencester to Andoversford Junction had been singled on 9 July 1928 when the original 75 lb per yd rail on the down line was lifted. It was 'life expired' and it was thought that a single track would suffice. On singling, some sections were realigned. This part of the railway was worked with the electric train token and the only intermediate crossing stations were Withington and Foss Cross. The signalboxes at Chedworth and Andoversford & Dowdeswell were abandoned. The up line from Andoversford & Dowdeswell to Andoversford was relegated to being a siding leading to Andoversford & Dowdeswell mileage sidings. These were worked by the 12.10 p.m. freight from Gloucester to Cirencester. Traffic had to be drawn to Dowdeswell and propelled from it.

To counteract road competition, the GWR opened halts in the 1930s at Chiseldon Camp[4] and Collingbourne Kingston[5], but on the debit side, stations at Blunsdon[6] and Andoversford & Dowdeswell[7], and Moredon Platform[8] for milk traffic, were closed. Andover & Dowdeswell was easily dispensed with, as it was only built because the MSW was not allowed at first to use the GWR's Andoversford station. It was the first time since the demobilisation after the first world war that trains had stopped at Chiseldon Camp, which since 1918 had been the Army Vocational Centre. Thirty soldiers used it on the opening day. Passengers for Ogbourne and Chiseldon paid on arrival at these stations, while other passengers paid either at Marlborough or at Swindon Town.

Earlier, on 2 February 1928, an agreement was made with the Southern Railway to provide locomotives for all troop specials to and from Ludgershall and Tidworth. This was more convenient than bringing down special engines from Swindon, though the MSW had always worked them to get the maximum receipts. A loop was actually pegged out at Ludgershall some time before the second world war which would have allowed through running from Tidworth to the north to avoid reversing at Ludgershall, but no further steps were taken.

On 6 April 1936 a supplementary streamlined diesel railcar service was introduced with a daily itinerary: Cheltenham St James, Swindon Town, Swindon Junction, Swindon Town, St James, Swindon Town, Savernake, Devizes, Swindon Town, Swindon Junction, Stroud, Gloucester and St James. It was soon withdrawn through lack of traffic, though it provided a fast service reaching 60 m.p.h. in places.

TEMPORARY RESURGENCE

The line became a strategic route again during the second world war, carrying wounded soldiers north and war supplies south, just as it had done in the first. Several times it was so jammed with traffic that everything ground nearly to a standstill, all crossing places and stations being occupied for hours on end with coal, freight and military trains in addition to the ordinary traffic.

During the evacuation from Dunkirk, seven troop trains were in Tidworth at once. They were brushed out at Ludgershall and sent back to Dover. One driver took No. 4377 over the whole length of main line with a 430 ton trainload of evacuated men; this was a remarkable feat as the normal loading for a through train was 368 tons. Apart from the special troop trains, servicemen used the line going to and from the camps on leave and while off duty, so that the ordinary passenger trains were packed. Many travelled to Swindon for entertainment.

In February 1941 traffic had grown to such proportions that Swindon control was opened, to look after the loading and regulation of freight trains and relief of trainmen on the MSW section. More siding accommodation was needed, and at Ludgershall a new military store siding was built on the west side of the line, controlled from a new ground frame. Perham South came into use on 3 January 1940. Also, an extension was put on the turntable at Ludgershall so that the long-wheelbased 28XX class engines need not be sent to Andover. The steel extensions were normally folded down out of the way, but when needed bars were put into holes and the extensions lifted up to rest on the surface of the running rails so that the pony truck could be carried out on the extension; the end of the extension curved up like a ski to prevent the wheels running off. The 2—8—0 engines were limited to hauling eighty empties between Tidworth and Ludgershall. Tidworth was very busy and would commonly have as many as 290 wagons in the yard.

The capacity of the main line was increased when the nine crossing loops north of Marlborough were extended at a cost of £53,000 between July 1942 and February 1943 to take longer freight trains. Some of the points were so far from the box that they were worked off a hand-turned generator. On 22 October 1942, Rushey Platt (MSW) up crossing loop was extended at the Cheltenham end for about 210 yd over the bridge—which had been built to carry double line, but which until then had never done so. At Chiseldon on 22 November 1942 the refuge siding, a truncated former siding to Chiseldon Camp, was converted to an additional up loop, 909 ft long, which with the up platform loop of 703 ft made a 1,600 ft crossing loop, holding an engine, seventy-nine wagons and brake van.

At Swindon Town 'B' signal box on 29 November 1942 a new up and down main line were put in, and the existing up and down main lines converted to up and down loops. A new Swindon Town South ground frame was opened 700 yd from 'B' box to control the exit from the down siding to the down main.

A new signal box was opened at Ogbourne on 7 January 1943 on the down side at 24m. 21ch., and the up and down loops were extended at the Swindon end. On 12 April the same year, at Chiseldon Camp halt a new up siding controlled by two ground frames ('North' and 'South'), both on the Swindon side of the halt, were brought into use, as well as an end-loading dock for armoured vehicles. An intermediate token instrument and telephone were installed for locking the train in. A train of warflats was constantly kept there for tank loading and had to be replaced when taken away. The 'North' and 'South' ground frames were taken out on 19 December 1950.

The line from Red Post Junction to Weyhill was doubled by the addition of an up line at a cost of £42,000 and a signal box opened at Red Post on 5 September 1943 1m. 383 yd west of Andover Junction West box. The up and down branch lines were connected with the up and down main lines at Red Post Junction, though most of the regular trains still used the original third road to Andover Junction. The Weyhill tablet instruments were transferred from the GWR Weyhill signal box to the SR Red Post box, the single-line section then being Andover Junction West to Red Post Junction. The junction at Red Post contravened the 1873 agreement, but from 1917 to 1936 a crossing loop and connection had been in existence.

Savernake Forest became a huge ammunition dump for storing explosives for D-Day. Entry to the ammunition sidings was controlled by North Savernake ground frame on the down side at 16m. 50ch. It was put in on 18 August 1943 and taken out in July 1950. In 1946 an ammunition train caught fire in these sidings: the blaze was confined to the rear wagons and the fireman went back as far as he could and uncoupled most of the train, which was drawn forward and saved, though it could not go on to the main line out of the way as the tablet was not available. The school train from Marlborough to Patney & Chirton on the BHE was in the section, and as the ammunition exploded this train stopped. The driver never understood quite why; he believed he must have instinctively applied the brake. Fortunately no one was injured.

In preparation for the landing in Normandy in 1944, a succession of approximately seventy special trains carried troops, armaments and supplies to the military areas on the Marlborough Downs and at Tidworth; the signal boxes had to be opened day and night. Fortunately the Great Western had strengthened the bridges in the early 1930s and heavier engines, including Ministry of Supply, 'Austerity' class and LMS 2—8—0s, were able to help work the traffic.

LAST DAYS

With nationalisation, the line first became part of the Western Region of British Railways, but from 2 April 1950 until 1 February 1958 it was divided between the Western and Southern Regions. The boundary was immediately north of Grafton station. The stations in the Southern Region were repainted green and SR upper-quadrant signals replaced some lower-quadrant types. The former MSW shed at Andover Junction was closed and at the beginning of 1953 SR engines based on Eastleigh and outshedded at Andover made their appearance.

As already said, the Tidworth branch was closed to passenger traffic on 19 September 1955 and the line worked by the War Department from 28 November 1955. Grafton Curve was rarely used and was closed on 5 May 1957. But the major blow came on 30 June 1958, when through services were reduced to one each way between Cheltenham and Andover. Track changes at Lansdown Junction, Cheltenham, later in the year robbed MSW trains of the route into Lansdown station, and from 3 November the surviving through train was diverted to Cheltenham St James. The three fitted freights each way were withdrawn, leaving no regular goods trains between Andoversford and Cirencester and only local freights south of Cirencester. From 15 September 1958 Savernake High Level was closed to passenger traffic and the MGR line from Grafton Junction to Marlborough (13m. 46ch.—19m. 25ch.) lifted in 1960.

The double track south of Ludgershall through Weyhill station to Red Post Junction became single from 29 August 1960. The main-line connection at Red Post was taken out and single-line working began between Andover Junction 'B' and Ludgershall, a distance of 7½ miles. The single-line tablet instrument at Red Post Junction was transferred to Ludgershall box, and Weyhill box closed and replaced by a ground frame.[9] The railway was now only a shadow of what it had been.

The final blow came in 1961 when it was announced that passenger trains from Andoversford Junction to Andover would be withdrawn from 9 September and the railway from Ludgershall to

Savernake, Marlborough to Swindon Town, and Cirencester (Watermoor) to Andoversford closed completely. Goods trains were still to run from Swindon to Cirencester and Swindon Town, from Andover to Ludgershall and Savernake to Marlborough. The stations at Ludgershall, Marlborough and Cricklade were to be kept open for parcels traffic. Andoversford to Dowdeswell became a siding.

The line from Cheltenham to Andover had been losing £113,000 a year; and an average of only eighty-nine passengers used Marlborough station daily, though this was probably the line's busiest station. All but twenty-five of this number were schoolchildren. Chiseldon station had a fair amount of traffic, twenty children using it daily, and often after a football match at Swindon as many as a hundred passengers leaving the train; but even this was a contrast to ten years earlier, when trains between Marlborough and Swindon were so crowded that passengers had to stand in the guard's van. Local opposition to closure was ineffective. The Transport Users' Consultative Committee said that a diesel service would not pay and the Wiltshire County Council accepted the alternative bus services for schoolchildren. Marlborough College was not greatly inconvenienced as its special train was still to run at the beginning and end of term.

As a final fling, on August Bank Holiday 1961, No. 7808 *Cookham Manor* pulled a regular train which had been increased to twelve coaches to cope with the traffic. On the last workmen's train from Swindon to Cirencester on 8 September a wreath was fixed to the engine. The following day the last regular run over the whole of the line, the 1.50 p.m. from Cheltenham, was pulled by an SR 2—6—0 locomotive. The Stephenson Locomotive Society ran a special over the MSW on 10 September pulled by *Cookham Manor*, and the Railway Correspondence & Travel Society ran a similar trip pulled by No. 5306. On this last day there was also the regular Sunday service of two trains each way between Swindon Junction and Andover.

The track was lifted from the closed sections—Ludgershall to Grafton and Cirencester to Andoversford in 1963, Marlborough to Swindon Town in 1964, Moredon to Cirencester in 1965—and some modern semi-detached houses south of Swindon Town goods yard promptly had their rates increased, as trains could no longer spoil their amenities.

The diesel-hauled goods which ran from Mondays to Fridays between Swindon and Cirencester was withdrawn from 1 April 1964, but coal trains are still worked to Moredon power-station siding when required, which is mainly in the winter as the power station is only a stand-by. Four goods trains ran to Marlborough each week until 19 May 1964 when Marlborough became a coal depot only. It was closed entirely 7 September 1964. From 19 May 1964 Swindon Town handled coal traffic and oil tanks for Esso only and from 1 November 1966 Esso oil tanks only on a private siding basis, the station being a private siding only.

When the Banbury & Cheltenham Direct Railway was lifted, 'Castles' and 'Halls' went up to Andoversford from Cheltenham to collect the rails, the first time these engines had used the line for many years. The very last train of rails to leave Andoversford ran on 23 December 1964, pulled by an ex-Midland engine, No. 43887.

The sole remains of the Midland & South Western today are the two short arms from Swindon[10] and the branch from Andover to Ludgershall.

CHAPTER 8

The Course of the Line

THE SOUTHERN END

The MSW began at Red Post Junction, but trains which did not run through to Southampton terminated at Andover. MSW trains normally used the outer face of the up island platform of Andover Junction, occasionally the up main. Beyond the east end of the platform the line made junctions with the LSW up and down slow lines, but not the through fast roads. The MSW engine shed was near, but separate from the LSW shed.

MSW trains took the independent third road, parallel to the LSW main line to Red Post, where they curved to the north. Here, at milepost 0, the MSW metals began. Red Post signal box was built during the first world war, abolished in 1936, re-erected during the second world war, and since demolished again.

Until 1943 the line as far as Weyhill was single. Weyhill held an important fair lasting three days every October which brought considerable traffic and to which the LSW, MR and GWR would send their canvassers. The station had seven sidings, a goods shed and a cattle-dock running off at an angle north-west. An area 120 yd by 17 yd was laid out for the temporary storage of cattle and sheep. As there were long sidings on two sides, loading and unloading could go on simultaneously; platelayers were drafted to help after the fair, the company providing cheese and a barrel of beer for their refreshment. On 10 October 1922 Weyhill fair brought receipts of £341 9s 10d to the MSW, which used 129 trucks—two engines spending the day shunting.

The two-road passenger station had the usual MSW-pattern nameplates of white enamel letters on a blue ground; plates giving the number of an over or under bridge were in the same style. The small enamel nameplates on the station lamps had white letters on a black ground; originally MSW stations and signal boxes were painted brown. The station, like most on the MSW, was built of brick. The line was level through the station and rose at 1 in 120 beyond. A nest of sidings was built for RAF use during the second world war.

As late as 1940 a horse was used to raise water from the well in the cattle dock:

> The pumps are actually at the bottom of a well, eighty feet down. The driving shaft has a large cog wheel fixed at the top end, which engages in a spur wheel attached to a fifteen-foot pole. This pole is harnessed to the horse who plods solemnly round and round, keeping the pumps in motion. Truly the 'daily round and common task'.[1]

Between Weyhill and Ludgershall the line passed near Appleshaw, where a small length of temporary railway was laid by the contractors for obtaining ballast when the line was built. A descent brought the railway to Ludgershall, the largest station on the line, covering sixteen acres. It had five platforms—two through roads with a bay on the up side for the Tidworth branch trains, which left at the north end, and a double road bay on the down side. The platform faces had a length of 3,942 ft. The bay line was lifted after the withdrawal of the passenger services to Tidworth in 1955. To accommodate general service wagons and baggage the platforms were spacious; they were connected by a covered lattice-girder footbridge. Any vehicle derailed at the catch-point in the goods yard depressed a pedal, which automatically released the wires of the up starting signal and up and down branch signals; it also rang a continuous warning bell in the signal box.

From the turn of the century the station was active with military traffic, and with civilian traffic during the time of the Tidworth Tattoo. When camps were occupied, beer was taken to Messrs Simmonds' Salisbury Plain depot. During the summer manoeuvres the staff at Ludgershall used to work twelve hours a day for six days a week, with only an hour or two's rest snatched in the waiting room. They were not paid a special rate on Sunday, being allowed time off in lieu. The station was extended between 1900 and 1902, a turntable and small engine shed being added. In 1901 a corrugated iron goods shed was erected at a cost of £400, at the north end of the yard by the turntable. Today a stop block ends the main line at the north end of the goods yard; beyond it the track has been lifted.

After climbing to Widgerly Down the train arrived at Collingbourne. The station was above the picturesque thatched village, and had three sidings and a horse dock. There was considerable racehorse traffic, and also agricultural machinery, as Messrs Rawlings & Sons' works adjoined the station. Beyond, the railway closely

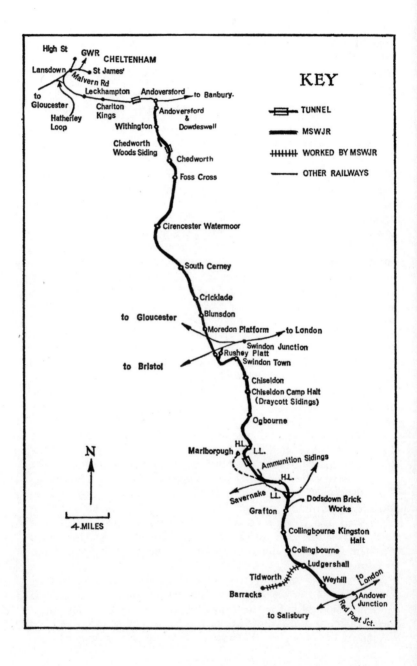

followed the River Bourne. Collingbourne Kingston halt, opened
1 April 1932, had two wooden platforms, built from sleepers, with
corrugated iron sheds. Tickets could be bought from a nearby house.
Beyond the halt the line rose at 1 in 150.

Grafton was a red-brick station relieved with grey glazed brick.
It had two sidings in addition to two sidings for a brickworks added
in 1898, and a cattle-loading stage. At one time an old van body on
the platform was used as a lamp room, but this burnt down and,
more wisely, the new one was built of brick and placed some
distance from the station. The station dealt with sixty to seventy
churns of milk daily.

North of Grafton was a cutting through greensand, which involved the removal of 33,000 cu. yd of material. Three-quarters of
a mile further on were two junctions; the Marlborough & Grafton
Railway kept straight ahead to Savernake High Level station, while
the other line curved westward to Savernake Low Level, and the
Grafton Curve bent east to the GWR giving a through run in the
direction of Newbury.

On the opening of the MGR, when the single-line connection
between Savernake Low Level and this southern section of the
MSW became superfluous, the junction was dismantled and the spur
left as a siding worked from a three-lever ground frame. On 1
November 1900 the junction was reinstated and a loop siding put in
for wagon transfers. A second loop siding was added, and Wolfhall
Junction box, owned by the MSW, was opened on 28 July 1902 to
control movements. The double-line Grafton Curve, 44 chains long,
was opened on 6 September 1905 under an agreement which gave
the Great Western running powers from Wolfhall Junction to
Ludgershall, and as already said in Chapter 4, Wolfhall Junction box
was moved further south where it could control both lines. It had a
forty-lever Sykes frame and Tyers three-position single-wire block
indicators. It was switched in for the through daily goods train
from the Great Western to Ludgershall and when required for goods
trains calling at Wolfhall, and also for special military and tattoo
trains. The Curve never had a regular passenger service. It was
closed on 5 May 1957. Wolfhall Junction exchange sidings were
very busy during the first world war, and sometimes a pilot engine
helped with the shunting and banked trains up the 1 in 106 through
Savernake station and in the other direction up the 1 in 109 to
Grafton.

The Kennet & Avon Canal ran under the platforms of Savernake
Low Level[2] in a tunnel 502 yd long. At this station the Marlborough

shuttle trains used the bay at the down end of the up platform. At one time there was a refreshment room managed by the nearby Forest Hotel. The platforms were lengthened, the footbridge roofed and red-brick waiting rooms built on the south platform for the opening of the Stert-Westbury line on 1 October 1900.

The High Level station (High Level was added to its name 1 July 1924) was about 200 yd north of the Low Level station. The Marquess of Ailesbury had a private waiting room on the down platform—as stipulated in the MGR's Act. A footbridge connected the platforms, each 500 ft long. The station was gay with flowers during the spring and summer, and lilacs, berberis and other shrubs still grow in the cutting. At one time there was a Wiltshire Farmers' milk depot in the station yard. In 1933 when the line was singled between Grafton South and Marlborough, the signal box became a ground frame for controlling the sidings. The station was closed to passengers on 15 September 1958 without any public notice having been given, and to goods on 22 June 1959.

The old Marlborough Railway climbed the hill below the MSW line and 1¾ miles north of the station was diverted into the up line of the MGR and what was once double track became two single lines, as mentioned in the last chapter. Until 1933 the double track ran all the way from Weyhill to Marlborough.

As the GWR Marlborough branch and the MGR were in sight of each other, and rivalry between the two companies was keen, trains leaving Marlborough together would often race to Savernake; the GWR usually won as it used only a two-coach train. (The Great Western used to call the line the 'Smack', and MSW men retaliated by referring to the GWR train as a 'Winkle Boat'.) Between Savernake and Marlborough the line skirted Savernake Forest.

Near the summit of the line, not far from the spot where the Marlborough Railway and the MGR converged at Hat Gate, was the site of the ammunition sidings laid during the last war by American troops. It was said that the ammunition dump in Savernake Forest was one of the biggest in Europe and 10,000 troops worked in the wired-off compound. A siding led off eastwards into the forest and branched into eight or nine roads.

Carved in the stone above the southern portal of the Marlborough Tunnel can still be seen the stone laid in 1898 by the Marchioness of Ailesbury. The tunnel, 647 yd, had to be relined in 1925 when the down line was temporarily interlaced with the up for about 30 ch (electric train tablet working was in operation between 4 January 1925 and 30 May 1926). Parts of it were again relined in

1944. Only the down line was used, with electric train token working between the temporary signal boxes between 26 July that year and 18 August 1946. The brickwork is now flaking badly. The chalk slopes of the 70 ft deep cutting have collapsed and now cover the site of the former down line. When the line was open, detritus had to be regularly shovelled away from the foot of the cuttings at both ends of the tunnel, and during hard weather a twenty-four-hour watch had to be kept. This tunnel has a place, albeit inglorious, in the annals of Marlborough College, as here groups of boys would smoke clandestine cigarettes. The gangers would sometimes give chase and try to secure the little black, black-ribboned caps which bore their school numbers. Rarely did they get either boy or cap.[3]

There followed a descent at 1 in 99 and a curve of 20 chains radius before Marlborough was reached. The junction with the GWR was removed on the opening of the MGR but restored in 1926. The High Level station (High Level added 1 July 1924), with its brick walls and stone surrounds to doors and windows, was seen to the west of the line, together with the Marlborough Railway engine shed. Many old employees still remember the time when an engine went through the back of the shed and provided material for teasing their GWR counterparts. For the twice-weekly pumping of water from the well into the tank above the shed the whistle was taken off to provide steam for working the pump engine outside the shed; the pump was coupled to the whistle, which was tied open. High Level was closed on 6 March 1933.

The Low Level station ('Low Level' added on 1 July 1924) had a refreshment room, and indeed it still has—a free house acting as a local for that end of the town. The refreshment rooms were once leased to the MSW stationmaster, but were transferred to the GWR Hotels & Refreshment Department in 1924. The original SMA signal box was at the Swindon end of the down platform; its brass handbell was rung when an approaching passenger train left Ogbourne or Savernake. It bore the company's initials, but the 'M' was cast upside down.

Marlborough dealt with an appreciable passenger traffic. In addition to boys going to and from Marlborough College, there were college visitors and traffic for Marlborough Fair; also Savernake Forest was a favourite resort on Bank Holidays and early-closing days. The goods yard had six sidings, a goods shed, horse dock and cattle pen. The horse dock was at the south end of the station off the down line, but as heavy motor traffic developed, the sudden noise of the vehicles going under the bridge frightened the horses

G

and the dock was moved to the north end of the up platform. There were training stables in the area and the horseboxes were attached to trains. The goods yard came into its own during the three sheep and cattle fairs. The station remained open for goods traffic after the withdrawal of the passenger service on 11 September 1961; it became a coal depot only from 19 May 1964 and was closed entirely on 7 September 1964.

Up trains left Marlborough's curved platform on a gradient of 1 in 75 down, and about halfway round the horseshoe bend the line crossed the River Kennet by a bridge with a span of 30 ft.

OVER THE MARLBOROUGH DOWNS

At Poulton Farm was a bridge of sarsen stones, one of several such bridges in the district. There used to be a spur which held about four horse boxes at Ogbourne St Andrew on the west side of the line. (Printed evidence of the existence of this siding is lacking, but a former MSW employee assured me it did exist.) Ogbourne had two sidings, a cattle pen and a horse dock used by racehorse traffic. The signal box used to be on the platform, but a new one was built north of the station when the loop was lengthened in 1943.

From Ogbourne until just before Chiseldon was a straight stretch of line parallel with a Roman road over bleak, open downland. Chiseldon Camp halt, opened 1 December 1930, was a sleeper platform with a corrugated iron shelter and was situated on the west side of the line, amid typical downland scenery. A 1½-mile long military siding extending from Chiseldon station was opened in September 1914. Draycott Camp, as it was known, had two wooden platforms and was later used as a demobilisation centre, capable of accommodating 3,000 men. Concrete 'pot'-type sleepers dating from the second world war still mark the site of the sidings which were opened on 12 April 1943. Chiseldon station itself—Chiseldon, as it was sometimes spelt—was in a cutting and had four sidings and a passing loop; again it dealt with racehorses. The line then passed Coate reservoir, formerly the property of the Wilts & Berks Canal. By the reservoir was an embankment 400-500 yd long with a maximum height of 32 ft, which required 200,000 tons of chalk and earth.

Swindon Town, known locally as Old Town, was in the centre of Swindon, but the town later developed in the direction of the GWR's station and works. Swindon Town at first had two platforms, but in 1904-5 was enlarged by making the up one into an island. It was

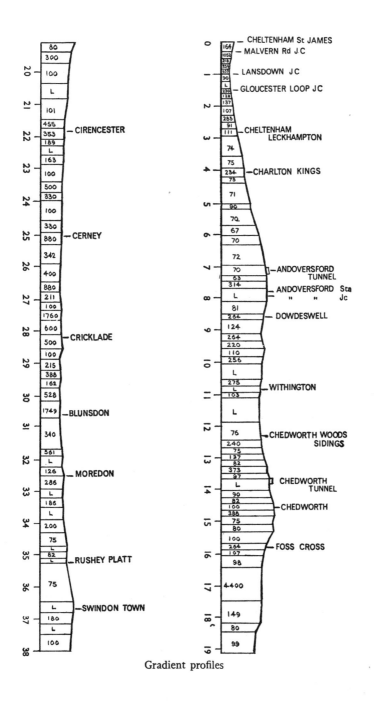

Gradient profiles

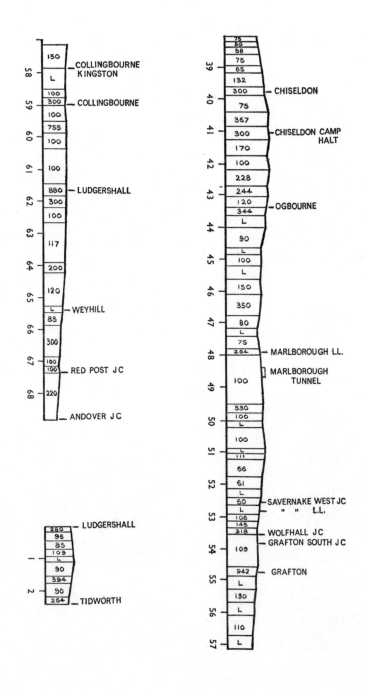

Left diagram (top):

Distance	Value	Location
58	150	COLLINGBOURNE KINGSTON
	L	
	100	
59	300	COLLINGBOURNE
	100	
60	755	
	100	
61	100	
62	880	LUDGERSHALL
	300	
	100	
63	117	
64	200	
65	120	
	L	WEYHILL
66	85	
	300	
67	100	
	100	RED POST JC
68	220	
		ANDOVER JC

Left diagram (bottom):

Distance	Value	Location
	280	LUDGERSHALL
	95	
	85	
1	109	
	L	
	90	
	394	
2	90	
	264	TIDWORTH

Right diagram:

Distance	Value	Location
39	75	
	80	
	98	
	75	
	65	
	132	
40	300	CHISELDON
	75	
41	367	
	300	CHISELDON CAMP HALT
	170	
42	100	
	228	
43	244	
	120	OGBOURNE
	344	
44	L	
	90	
45	L	
	100	
46	L	
	150	
	350	
47	80	
	L	
	75	
48	264	MARLBOROUGH L.L.
49	100	MARLBOROUGH TUNNEL
	330	
50	100	
	L	
	100	
51	L	
	111	
	66	
52	61	
	L	
	60	SAVERNAKE WEST JC
53	L	" " L.L.
	106	
	145	
	318	WOLFHALL JC
54	109	GRAFTON SOUTH JC
55	942	GRAFTON
	L	
	130	
56	L	
	110	
57	L	

the second largest station on the line, with platform faces totalling 1,548 ft, and was situated on a sharp curve. The outer face of the up island platform was used by the shuttle trains to Swindon Junction. Up and down sides were connected by a footbridge. A refreshment room was on the down platform and remained open after closure to passenger traffic until January 1965. The down platform had a well-kept garden, overlooked by The Croft, where the head offices were situated. Originally a centre road ran between the up and down through roads. The story is told that one night a shunter who had suffered the wrath of the stationmaster carefully left a truckload of calves on this centre road, directly in front of the stationmaster's bedroom, to await collection by the early-morning goods.

Swindon Town A box was at the up end of the station and Swindon Town B at the down end by the locomotive shed, with double-line block working between them. As the station was by the cattle market it had a cattle pen and horse dock as well as a goods shed, 55 ft turntable and water tower. The original engine shed was close to the south end of the station and when the island platform was put in, a new shed was built further south. On the up side were the engineering shops and a sheet repairing depot. The station is still open for oil.

A gradient of 1 in 75, the worst on the line, led down for $1\frac{1}{2}$ miles to Rushey Platt; southbound goods trains sometimes required banking. After the morning local goods from Swindon Junction to Swindon Town had finished shunting at Rushey Platt, the Swindon Town shunter would pilot it up the bank. Rushey Platt station (opened 1 December 1883, closed 1 October 1905) was just south of the bridge by which the MSW crossed the GW's main line. There were platforms both on the original SMA line to Swindon Junction and on the Cheltenham extension; the former can still be seen[4], and as late as 1935 trains would still unofficially stop to allow people using the station as a house to alight. The high-level platforms on the Cheltenham line were connected by a subway, blocked up in 1907 but still traceable just south of the signal box.

Rushey Platt was once important for milk traffic (the Low Level platform became a milk platform after cessation of passenger traffic) and indeed Rushey Platt to Cirencester was milk country just as Marlborough to Swindon was racehorse country. The two sidings in the timber yard at Rushey Platt are still used.

Under the original agreement, wagons were transferred to the Great Western east of the GWR Swindon station, the MSW working these transfer trips, but from the end of 1891 traffic was exchanged at Rushey Platt, each company working there. On 16 January 1922 the GWR started working transfer goods trains through to Swindon Town.

The GWR was crossed by a bridge of wrought-iron plate girders of 92½ ft span resting on masonry abutments, and then the line descended again at 1 in 75, becoming single after crossing the Wootton Bassett road. On the embankment close to the GWR line were three signals for sighting tests; these were worked from an adjoining ground frame. The embankment north of here gave trouble to the contractors when it slipped, causing the opening to be postponed. The MSW then passed the west end of the GWR scrapyard and went under the Cheltenham & Great Western Union Railway.

Moredon Platform (opened 25 March 1913, closed 1 October 1932) was on the south side of the road bridge and on the west side of the line and is still marked by a mound. The platform was opened specially to deal with milk traffic; receipts in 1922 totalled £819. The sidings to Moredon power station, formerly Swindon Corporation Electricity Works, are still used (opened 17 January 1928), their access being through a loop on GWR 1931 steel sleepers, with a two-lever ground frame at each end. Around 1950, 100 trucks of coal a day went to the power station, but quantities have fallen off in recent years.

Blunsdon, marked by a mound on the west side of the line north of the overbridge, is a good example of a wayside station which earned its keep during an era very different from ours—when milk was despatched by the churn to distant destinations instead of collected by lorries based on a centralised creamery. Opened 1 September 1895, it shared a stationmaster with Moredon and handled substantial cake, hay and straw traffic, though never many passengers. In 1913, passenger receipts were only £5, but parcels brought in £922 and goods £175. The siding, worked by a ground frame, had so sharp a curve that locomotives were not allowed to leave the main line, and guards had to make sure that trains were long enough to reach back to wagons to be collected. Weekday services ceased from 10 July 1922, after which Blunsdon was curiously served by one passenger train a week, a Sunday afternoon service which called principally for the milk traffic. It had the generous allowance of 45 min for the 8½ miles from Cricklade to Swindon Town. It ceased from 28 September 1924. The Gloucester goods called daily until 1936, and the station was closed to all traffic on 1 August 1937.

Cricklade station had a loop, four sidings, a goods shed, horse dock, cattle pens and a milk-loading platform; also, at one time, a beautiful bank of roses. The porter at Cricklade was busy enough, meeting trains, sorting eighty to a hundred churns daily, filling and cleaning lamps, and sheeting and roping wagons of hay and straw. Goods traffic lingered on after the withdrawal of passenger services in 1961, but came to an end on 1 July 1963. North of the station the line crossed the infant Thames by a span of 35 ft, with an opening of 11 ft 6 in. on the left bank allowing communication between the fields on either side of the railway. In the 1890s only two of the four girders were in position, the other two left unsecured ready for doubling; the line between Swindon and Cirencester was never doubled and they were later removed.

Soon the line passed lakes formed by gravel working and the ascent of the Cotswolds began. South Cerney originally had only one platform but another was added later. A goods loop in addition to the passing loop was opened in September 1900, and there was also a horse dock and three sidings. Sometimes 2—6—0 No. 16 came out from Swindon with a brake van to pick up ten to fifteen trucks of gravel from the sidings. The gravel had been dug up by hand, shovelled into a two-wheeled, horse-drawn cart, taken to the station and shovelled into the open wagons—a laborious task. The station has had two changes of title: originally Cerney & Ashton Keynes, it became just Cerney until 1 July 1924, when it was amended to South Cerney. Freight traffic was withdrawn on 1 July 1963.

After crossing the Thames & Severn Canal at Siddington, Ciren-ester (Watermoor) was reached. 'Watermoor' was added to its title on 1 July 1924, the same day as 'Town' was added to the name of the other GWR station at Cirencester. The principal railway build-ings were here, together with an extensive goods yard and engine shed. The station was stone-faced, in contrast to the red brick general on the line. In the spring of 1960, a mechanical digger hit and damaged the underline bridge north of the station, making the up line unsafe. From then onwards only the down line was used. Watermoor signal box, a tall wooden building, was taken out of service from 21 August 1960[5], and a ground frame was used for working sidings and allowing the engine to run round the terminat-ing trains; so one of the principal stations was no longer a block post. After the withdrawal of passenger services in 1961, the line north of the station was removed and buffer stops installed just beyond the platform. The station was finally closed to goods from 1 April 1964.

Leaving Cirencester, the line curved towards Fairford, originally to be served by a branch line, and cut through the Roman wall and earthwork at the Beeches. Then followed a straight stretch which gave a fast run for down trains and a welcome rest for firemen, for the MSW was a hard line to work. North of the bridge over the Foss Way the railway was carried across the Calmsden Valley by an embankment 59 ft high.

Foss Cross was a station far from houses, but passengers came from Bibury and Coln Rogers, especially in summer when going on their holidays. It handled almost as much goods traffic as did Cirencester; agricultural produce, timber and coal provided the main income. The station building had no platform canopy; quite a few other MSW stations had these added by the GWR. But Foss Cross boasted a goods shed and cattle pen, passing loop, two sidings and two more long ones for a quarry and stone-crushing plant to the south, which supplied ballast for the whole line—there were ballast holes on both sides of the station. The stone was not of very good quality, soon crumbling to dust, but had the advantage of being cheap—the quarry was owned by the MSW. When the Tidworth barracks were being built, many ballast trains travelled thence from Foss Cross, fourteen to twenty wagons a day leaving the quarry at peak periods.

A double-acting catch point at Foss Cross was in the bad winter of 1947 the cause of a snowplough being derailed; sometimes the snow at this isolated spot was so deep that the signalman slept the night in his box. Firemen found the air noticeably colder when they leaned out to catch the tablet. During the second world war an ambulance train taken to Foss Cross for stabling had to be divided as one siding was not long enough to hold it. The train was composed of LNE stock and the staff had never encountered the buckeye coupler before; it took them an hour to fathom how to uncouple the coaches.

North of the station the gradient steepened from 1 in 260 to 1 in 100 and about halfway to Chedworth the railway passed through an old quarry and reached the summit, 637½ ft above sea level. It then descended from the open downland to the sheltered Chedworth valley. Chedworth station was a timber building opened 1 October 1892, later than the other stations on the line, with one 180 ft platform sited on a curve. When the line was doubled, an up plat-

MSW LOCOMOTIVES—3

(26) *No. 11 with stovepipe chimney at Swindon*
(27) *No. 11 again, at Swindon with iron-capped chimney*

MSW LOCOMOTIVES—4

(28) *No. 14 at Swindon*
(29) *No. 16 'Galloping Alice' at Swindon*

MSW LOCOMOTIVES—5

(30) *No. 15 at Andover*
(31) *No. 17 at Swindon Town*

MSW LOCOMOTIVES—6

(32) *No.* 13 *at Swindon Town*

(33) *No.* 25

form was added, but on singling all trains reverted to using the down platform. Originally a signal box was at the down end of the up platform, but it was only opened when specially required, being worked by the stationmaster; in later years it was switched in only when a goods train had to call at Chedworth Woods sidings, and latterly it was abolished. The station became an unstaffed halt from 1 February 1954.

North of the station was Chedworth Tunnel, 491 yd long, with a stone portal at the south end visible from the village and improving the appearance of its high green hillside; the north portal, tucked away out of sight, was of much more workaday blue brick. It had a brick arch throughout, but the side walls were partly brick and partly natural rock. Since track lifting in 1963 the portals have been partially bricked up. Above the south portal is a ruined farmhouse and a dip in front of it marks the tunnel slip which delayed the line's opening. The tunnel was about 140 ft below the surface of the ground.

North of the tunnel is the Roman villa, discovered by rabbits which brought bits of tesselated pavement to the surface. The line passed through a steep-sided limestone cutting and, beyond, a wide embankment marked the spot of the two Chedworth Woods sidings, worked from a ground frame electrically controlled from Withington; there is still a trace of the 100 ft wooden platform. The siding was put in at the end of the 1914-18 war by the Timber Supply Department of the Board of Trade to remove several thousand tons of timber. Deer sometimes ran across the line by Withington Woods; this was a particularly scenic stretch.

Withington station, renamed 'Withington (Glos)' on 1 July 1924, had a horse-dock and a goods siding in the form of a loop. The crossing loop and signal box closed on 28 May 1956 when the station became an unstaffed halt. In later MSW days when the track north of Cirencester was double, the signal box was only open for stopping goods trains.

Andoversford & Dowdeswell station[6] was built by the MSW because until 1 October 1904 its trains were not allowed to stop at the GWR Andoversford station. It had a goods shed, cattle pen, two sidings and a horse-dock siding. The passenger station closed on 1 April 1927. When the track was singled, the original up line was left between Dowdeswell and Andoversford Junction as a goods siding and goods traffic continued until 15 October 1962 when the Banbury & Cheltenham Direct Railway was closed.

The junction with B & CDR was east of Andoversford station. The station had two signal boxes—Andoversford Station and Andoversford Junction. By the latter were two exchange sidings.

From the Cheltenham end of the yard there was a steep fall down the scarp of the Cotswolds and this 3½ miles of 1 in 63-72 to Charlton Kings limited the length of trains: on the MSW proper the ruling gradient was 1 in 75. 0—6—0 Beyer Peacock engines were limited to sixteen 10-ton wagons and the North British 4—4—0s to eighteen wagons. Andoversford Tunnel, west of the station, was 384 yd long and lined with blue brick. Crossing a lane at the River Chelt was a red-brick twelve-arch viaduct 543 ft long with arches of 40 ft span, and a maximum height of 70 ft. The mortar was made from blue clay and ballast and set like iron; when the contractor wished to take off a few courses of the piers after a severe frost, it was found that the bricks and mortar were impossible to separate. The newer bricks marking the widening in 1902 (Chapter 6) can be noticed. There were two continuous landslips by the viaduct and eleven altogether between Andoversford and Leckhampton. Not far from the viaduct the line ran parallel to a reservoir for about half a mile and made a splendid approach to Cheltenham.

Charlton Kings had wooden buildings and became a halt on 9 April 1956. It had been closed to goods on 1 December 1954. Leckhampton was a typical GWR brick suburban station, situated in a cutting with goods yard and attractive garden. There was formerly a 1¼-mile long mineral line from the station to Leckhampton Hill quarries; it was worked until its closure, about 1927, by *Lightmoor*, an 0—4—0 Peckett saddle-tank engine.[7]

One-and-a-half miles beyond the station was a triangular junction, Cheltenham trains taking the right-hand leg joining the GWR and MR Gloucester-Cheltenham line near the place where the MR diverged to Lansdown station. The left leg, Hatherley loop, gave a through run to Gloucester. This loop was opened on 1 January 1906 and from May that year until 1939 was used by the Newcastle-Swansea trains coming off the GCR and BCD route. The Gloucester to Swindon Town goods also used the loop. It fell into disuse after the second world war.

MSW passenger trains worked to and from Lansdown—using the through platforms as well as the bay on the east side—but running powers extended to High Street station to the north. Coaching stock was stored immediately north of Lansdown station, and two MSW parcels vans were kept in the dock at Lansdown. The goods sidings, eight exchange and two joint, were at High Street.

The MSW formed its own trains with its own engines; its engine shed (closed in 1935) alongside the exchange sidings held fourteen locomotives. Total MSW passenger receipts for Lansdown in 1921 were £5,066. A notice on the platform by the tea room used to read: 'Change here for Swindon, Marlborough, Andover, Portsmouth, Southampton, Cherbourg and France.'

CHAPTER 9

Working the System

Services began in July 1881 with six trains running daily each way between Swindon Town and Marlborough, and two on Sundays, taking about 30 minutes for the distance of 11¼ miles. The time allowed was found to be inadequate, and from the following month trains were allowed another 5 minutes. An extra late train ran each way on Saturdays for the benefit of revellers who had visited the market. Special market tickets were issued for journeys to Bath and Bristol. With the opening of the line to Swindon GWR station in February 1882, six trains ran through to Marlborough, taking about 40 minutes for the run, and one each way terminated at Swindon Town.

Grafton to Andover services began with four trains each way, except on Sundays, taking about 45 minutes to cover the 14¼ miles. One up and two down trains were mixed, as until through services could be arranged traffic did not warrant separate goods trains. After the GWR had put the Marlborough Railway in order, seven trains ran from Swindon to Andover Junction and on to Southampton, five starting from the GWR station at Swindon; the seven up trains all ran through to the GWR station. Two trains ran each way on Sundays. Most took 1h. 45m., though one completed the journey in 1h. 32m. One down train ran from Swindon GWR to Marlborough, but there was no corresponding up working. The Swindon to Cirencester services began with five trains each way and two on Sundays, taking about 30 minutes for the trip; the first train daily started from Rushey Platt, the rest from Swindon Town. A mixed train left Andover at 9.50 a.m., and arrived at Swindon Town at 1.15 p.m. The corresponding down train left at 4.20 p.m. and arrived at Andover at 7.40. For the opening to Cheltenham three trains ran each way, soon increased to four down from Cheltenham and five up, one of the latter being mixed. In the early days there was no Sunday service north of Swindon except for milk. Throughout the MSW's history great emphasis was of course laid on developing through traffic. In July 1891, three trains ran between Cheltenham and Andover, one down train with four stops taking only 2h. 5m. overall. Another was a mixed train taking 3h. 18m.; this had no corresponding up working, all the up services being ordinary stopping trains taking 2h. 50m.

On 1 June 1893, Fay utilised the important running powers to Southampton for passenger trains; these had been exercised by goods trains from 1 November 1892. Through coaches from Sheffield started in the summer of 1893 and the principal expresses were known as either the North or South Express. Through coaches were run daily between Bradford, Leeds, Sheffield, Derby, Liverpool, Birmingham and Southampton, the MSW providing the shortest route between these places. Old employees remember a Highland Railway van which ran regularly between Scotland and Southampton. Through coaches also ran between Cheltenham and Portsmouth. A large notice-board at Andover Junction invited LSW passengers to change for fast trains to Birmingham and the north. By August 1898 through services between Cheltenham and Andover had increased to six down and five up trains with an additional one each way on Saturdays. On Sundays two through up trains were run, but none in the down direction.

The opening of the MGR reduced the time between Marlborough and Savernake from 12 min to 9 and the distance was reduced by 31 chains. In October 1905 there were five through down trains taking from 2 hours to 3h. 15m. and seven up trains varying from 1h. 46m. by the North Express ('Horses and carriages not conveyed by this train') to 3h. 3m. The solitary Sunday down train took 3h. 20m. and left Cheltenham at the early hour of 6 a.m.; the up train took 2h. 53m. In 1905 through carriages ran to Southampton from Bradford, Leeds, Derby (two trains), Burton-on-Trent (two), Birmingham (two) and Cheltenham (four). From Southampton through carriages ran to Sheffield, Burton (two), Derby (two) and Cheltenham. In addition there were various short trains from Cirencester to Andover, Swindon to Andover, Swindon to Chiseldon and Andover to Tidworth.

In October 1910 a Manchester-Southampton coach was put on the South Express and on 1 May 1911 an accelerated and improved service from Manchester to Southampton was introduced. This same month the six through down trains were taking between 2h. 5m. and 3h. 5m. between Cheltenham and Andover and the six up trains were taking 1h. 49m. to 3h. 15m.—the latter being a mixed train between Andover and Swindon. One through down train ran on Sundays, taking 2h. 49m., and three up trains—the North Express covering the distance in 2h. 7m. Through carriages ran between Southampton and Nottingham, Burton, Birmingham, Manchester, Stockport and Crewe. From July to September 1913, 13,835 passengers were carried from stations north of Cheltenham to stations south of Andover and during the same period passenger-traffic earnings provided about 52 per cent of the company's revenue.

August 1914 marked the peak of MSW services, with weekend trains of eight or nine coaches. Two South Expresses were run to Southampton, one from Birmingham and the other from Manchester (London Road). Six through trains ran between Cheltenham and Southampton. The second of the two North Expresses stopped only at Swindon covering the distance in 105 minutes. On Sundays two trains ran each way with the addition of the North Express.

In October the same year the seven through down trains were taking between 1h. 51m. and 3h. 9m., and the seven up trains from 1h. 49m. to 3h. 28m. Two down trains ran on Sundays. The first left Cheltenham at 5.15 a.m. and was mixed as far as Ciren-cester, where it stayed for 48 min. It took 4h. 5m. for the journey from Cheltenham to Andover, the other train taking 2h. 49m. The three up trains were faster, the North Express taking 2h. 4m. and the others 2h. 18m. and 2h. 31m. In July 1915, two trains ran to Chiseldon and back, with an additional seven on Saturdays.

The war caused the cessation of through carriages. When they were resumed in 1922, the Southampton to Manchester coach was diverted to Liverpool and the second through service was reduced to a semi-fast between Cheltenham and Southampton; the total of forty weekday trains and twenty Sunday trains of October 1913 had fallen to thirty-three and two respectively. The last MSW time-table, issued in July 1923, gives four through down trains, taking from 2h. 13m. to 3h. 23m., and four up trains taking from 2h. 5m. to 3h. 6m. No through down trains ran on Sundays. Other trains ran over intermediate distances, including a mixed train from Swindon to Chiseldon.

On 22 October 1923 the GWR restored the Swindon Town-Swindon Junction shuttle service after an absence of thirty-nine years. Discontinued on 21 September 1925, only to be restored again within six months, it was locally known as the 'Old Town Bunk', the 'Dodger', or the 'Loop' train. And from 9 July 1928 to 18 July

1932 a 9.10 a.m. Mondays-only market passenger train ran from Foss Cross to Gloucester.

The GWR continued the through coach from Liverpool (Lime Street) to Southampton until the outbreak of war in 1939, when there were still four through trains from Cheltenham to Andover, the fastest in the up direction taking 2h. 9m. The GWR generally lengthened the time allowance; the MSW allowed 12 min between Ludgershall and Andover, and the GWR 15 min. From 1 October 1941 the 2 p.m. Cheltenham-Southampton, the old South Express and the 2.35 p.m. Andover-Cheltenham were withdrawn, leaving the line poorly served with through connections. Passenger accommodation on the surviving trains was in three to five coaches, which were well filled and sometimes crammed to bursting point with troops as well as civilians.

In October 1947 the three down trains took from 2h. 45m. to 3h. and the three up trains 2h. 20m. to 2h. 52m. The 7 a.m. milk empties from Andover Junction to Swindon Town ran as a mixed train from Savernake Low Level to Marlborough. A mixed train ran in the evening from Marlborough to Savernake Low Level and was allowed 22 min instead of 11 as wagon brakes had to be pinned down at the gradient board.

In 1955 there were still three trains each day between Cheltenham and Andover, the fastest taking 2h. 26m., in addition to others over shorter distances such as Swindon-Andover, the 'Dodger' and the Marlborough-Savernake shuttle service. Two trains ran each way between Swindon Junction and Andover on Sundays.

A drastic cut on 30 June 1958 left only one through train a day. The up train took 3h. 2m. and the down 2h. 46m. During the last three years of the line's existence, the timings on Sundays, south of Swindon, were much more convenient than on weekdays, especially for passengers wishing to spend some hours on the south coast. On Sundays particularly, the cheap tickets to Southsea and Bournemouth were well patronised until closure.

SPECIAL SERVICES

In July 1893 an Ocean Boat Express ran from various places in the north to Southampton and continued to work until 1914. At one time a through train from Whitehaven was run for the benefit of emigrants from Cumberland's newly-depressed industrial area. Another train carried to Southampton emigrants from Italy, the Ukraine, Bulgaria and Rumania, as well as Britain, who gathered at

Liverpool. It ran every Friday morning, sometimes in two parts. Many of the families had two or three children and were a pitiful sight, with their few belongings. Mugs of coffee and bags of biscuits were put on luggage trucks at Cheltenham (Lansdown) station for them. At Southampton the train ran into the docks alongside the boat and the MSW canvassing agent would check off the passengers; they all wore card identity-discs round their necks, and his job was made more difficult by the fact that the children had often chewed theirs and rendered them illegible. The trains reeked of garlic and had to be fumigated before further use. From July to September 1913, 2,891½ emigrants were carried.

Each Tuesday and Friday, an express to the docks was provided for passengers by the American Lines and White Star Lines to New York and by the Union Castle boats to the Cape, etc. The train could be stopped at any station between Cheltenham and Andover for any ocean-going passenger if twenty-four hours' notice was given. But this boat train was not reintroduced after the first world war. The MSW agent would tour the Southampton hotels to persuade passengers for the north to use the MSW route.

A special train was run at the beginning of each school term from Paddington to Marlborough, and in addition a special through coach from Waterloo, which was attached at Andover to the last up train to Swindon. The end of term brought no corresponding service to Waterloo, the only through coaches running to Paddington. In recent times this train was hauled by a 55xx 2—6—2 tank engine to Swindon Junction and thence by a 'Castle'.

The first royal journey over the MSW took place on 16 November 1899, when HRH Princess Henry of Battenburg travelled from Cirencester to Cheltenham. Outside the entrance to the waiting-room at Watermoor, a porch was built of white and royal-blue drapery surmounted by a crown, and decorated with a shield and trophy of flags. The train was drawn by one of the company's newest express engines and consisted of the royal saloon, a first-class saloon and a guard's van.

PASSENGER FACILITIES

Family saloons and invalid carriages were available for use at forty-eight hours' notice, except on certain expresses, and compartments could be reserved for ladies only. And the timetables stated: 'For convenience of Gentlemen Hunting in the vicinity of the Line, Return Tickets for Horses will be issued at a reduced charge of

MSW 0—6—0s IN ACTION

(34) *No. 22 with passenger train near Stockbridge* (LSW); *bogie coach and two six-wheelers. Right-hand buffer missing*

(35) *No. 26 with goods train, c.*1914

MSW LOCOMOTIVES IN THE GWR ERA—1

(36) *No. 1119 with double-domed boiler at Swindon Junction*
(37) *No. 1120 after rebuilding*

One Fare and one-half at Owner's risk. The Horses may return the same or following day.' Luncheon baskets were supplied at Swindon Town, and tea baskets, 6d apiece, at Swindon and Marlborough; telegrams could be sent ahead free of charge, ordering these or other refreshments to be brought to the train on its arrival.

Two pages of the Summer Excursion Programme for 1901 are reproduced. It will be noted that the fare price depended on the station group and the length of stay: for example, the fare to Waterloo from Gloucester, Cheltenham, Dowdeswell, Withington or Chedworth was 9s for four days, 11s for five days and 12s for eight, eleven, twelve or fifteen days. Cheap tickets were available from MSW stations to most of the principal stations in the British Isles (though, significantly, not to places on the GWR) and also to the Channel Islands, various French destinations and Dublin (*via* Liverpool). Tourists from Cheltenham to places in East Anglia were routed *via* Andover, Waterloo and either the Great Northern or the Great Eastern—they travelled almost twice as many miles as by the direct route. Locally, combined rail and coach trains could be arranged for six or more people, on application. On Mondays a Savernake Forest drive was offered, on Tuesdays a Cotswold Hills drive, on Wednesdays a drive to Fairford to see the fine stained-glass windows in the church, on Fridays a drive to Seven Springs, and on Saturdays a drive to Stonehenge.

As mentioned earlier, the MSW would allow expresses to be stopped at intermediate stations if advance notice was given. However, on 29 June 1900 a memo was sent from the general manager's office to all stationmasters:

SPECIAL STOPPAGES OF TRAINS

Now that the busy season is upon us, you must, in every instance of an application being made to you for trains to be stopped specially at any Station, deprecate the same in every possible way, by pointing out that, while the Company is always ready to assist the convenience of passengers so far as they can, yet, the margins at Andover Jc. and Cheltenham respectively are so narrow, that any interference with the running of the trains jeopardises these connections, and when missed, result in extreme inconvenience to through passengers and other traffic. You must only refer to me in cases that are exceptionally special, and decline all others.

About 1911 an American millionaire missed his boat at Southampton and, hearing that another was sailing from Liverpool, ordered a special train to take him there. It consisted of a brake composite pulled by No. 9. The driver made good speed to Cheltenham and received a worthwhile tip.

H

Summer Excursion Programme & Tourist Arrangements,

1901.

FOR GENERAL CONDITIONS SEE PAGE 6.

1st, 2nd & 3rd Class Tourist Tickets, available for two Calendar Months, will be issued until further notice.

Every FRIDAY and MONDAY, until further notice, a Cheap Excursion Train will run to ·

LONDON

WATERLOO, VAUXHALL, QUEEN'S ROAD, CLAPHAM JUNCTION, and *via* CLAPHAM JUNCTION to CHELSEA, WEST BROMPTON, KENSINGTON (Addison Road), SHEPHERD'S BUSH, HAMMERSMITH (The Grove), and RAVENSCOURT PARK, *via* ANDOVER JUNCTION, as under:—

Leaving	Times.	Third Class Return Fares.			Leaving	Times.	Third Class Return Fares.		
		Four Days.	Five Days.	8, 11, 12 or 15 Days.			Four Days.	Five Days.	8, 11, 12 or 15 Days.
	p.m.					p.m.			
Tewkesbury dep.	12 14				Swindon Town dep.	4 3			
Ashchurch "	12 19				Chiseldon "	2 38	7/6	8/6	8/6
Gloucester "	12 22				Ogbourne "	2 47			
Cheltenham "	3 0	9/-	11/-	12/-					
Dowdeswell "	1 32				Marlborough "	4 31			
Withington "	1 37				Savernake "	4 41	6/6	7/6	7/6
Chedworth "	1 44				Grafton "	3 13			
Cirencester "	3 40				Collingbourne "	3 22			
Cerney "	2 3	8/-	9/6	9/6	Ludgershall "	4 57	6/-	6/6	6/6
Cricklade "	2 11				Weyhill "	3 38			

Passengers booked on Fridays return the following Monday (4 days), Friday (8 days), Monday week (11 days) or Friday week (15 days). Passengers booked on Mondays return the following Friday (5 days), Monday (8 days), Friday week (12 days) or Monday week (15 days), as under :—

	Fridays.	Mondays.		Fridays.	Mondays.		Fridays.	Mond'ys
	a.m.	a.m.		a.m.	a.m.		a.m.	a.m.
Waterloo dep.	8.5	7.10	Clapham Junction .. dep. 8.14	7.22		Kensington (Addison Road) dep. 7.20	6.58
Vauxhall "	8.0	7.15	Ravenscourt Park .. " 7.13		West Brompton	" 7.23	7.1
Queen's Road "	7.53	6.54	Hammersmith (The Grove) " 7.18		Chelsea	" 7.35	7.3
			Shepherd's Bush " 7.20				

Passengers cannot return from Ravenscourt Park, Hammersmith, and Shepherd's Bush on Mondays.

Waterloo Station is within a few minutes' walk of the Houses of Parliament, Westminster Abbey, and Principal Theatres. Trains run every five minutes between Waterloo and Charing Cross, Cannon Street and London Bridge. Electrical Trains run between Waterloo and the City on week days every few minutes from 7.30 a.m. until 10 p.m. ; fares, single 2d., return 3d. ; thus giving quick and direct access to the City from Waterloo Station Platform.

Similar Tickets will be issued from London to Stations on the M. & S.W. Junction Railway on every Friday and Monday thereafter until further notice. For Particulars see London and South Western Co.'s Programme.

CHEAP EXCURSION TRAINS TO

WORCESTER, BIRMINGHAM & WOLVERHAMPTON

FOR 1, 2 or 3 DAYS, will run as under:—

Every WEDNESDAY and SATURDAY until further notice, except Saturdays, Aug. 3 & 10:—

Fares, Third Class Return.

From	a.m.	To Worcester. Two or Three Days.	Birmingham· & Wolverhampton Two or Three Days.
Andover Jn.	9.15		
Weyhill	9.23		
Ludgershall	9.32	7/-	7/-
Collingb'rne	9.38		
Grafton	9.47		
Savernake	9.54		
Marlborough	6.28		
Ogbourne	6.41	6/-	6/-
Chiseldon	6.53		
Swindon	7.15		
Rushey Platt	7.20	6/-	6/-
Blunsdon	7.29		
Cricklade	7.37	4/9	5/6
Cerney	7.45	4/3	5/6

Return Time Table for Passengers booked from above Stations EACH WEDNESDAY—

	From Wolverhmptn.	Birmingham.	Worcester
Thursday or Friday	1.22 p.m.	3.34 p.m.	3.10 p.m.

EACH SATURDAY—

	From Wolverhmptn.	Birmingham.	Worcester
Sunday	8.45 a.m.	10.12 a.m.	10.12 a.m.
Monday or Tuesday	1.22 p.m.	3.34 p.m.	3.10 p.m.

Every THURSDAY and SATURDAY until further notice, except Saturdays, Aug. 3 & 10:—

Fares, Third Class Return.

From	a.m.	To Worcester. Two or Three Days. Day Trip.		Birmingham & Wolverhampton Two or Three Days. Day Trip.		Wolverhmptn. Two or Three Days. Day Trip.	
Cirencester ..	8.3						
Foss Cross ...	8.16						
Chedworth ..	8.20	3/3	4/3	4/3	4/9	4/3	6/-
Withington ...	8.27						
Andoversford &							
Dowdeswell	8.32						

Return Time Table for Passengers booked from above Stations on

EACH THURSDAY—

	Wolverhampton.	Birmingham.	Worcester.
Thursday ..	5.10 p.m.	7.18 p.m.	6.57 p.m.
Friday or Saturday	5.10 "	7.18 "	6.57 "

EACH SATURDAY—

	From Wolverhmptn.	Birmingham.	Worcester.
Saturday ..	5.10 p.m.	7.18 p.m.	6.57 p.m.
Sunday	8.45 a.m.	8.45 a.m.	10.12 a.m.
Monday or Tuesday	5.10 p.m.	7.18 p.m.	6.57 p.m.

(1)

Two pages from comprehensive summer excursion programme, 1901

A Holiday in the Cotswold Country and North Wilts.

OUT of the beaten track of British tourists, the breezy downs and verdant dales lying between Cheltenham and Andover, now made easily accessible by the railway Stephenson projected 45 years ago, under the high-sounding title of the "Manchester and Southampton Direct," give us, nevertheless, all that the rest-seeking and holiday-making excursionist can desire. To-day one of the most thinly-peopled districts in England, evidence abound of a more than average population in Roman and prehistoric times. Quaint villages, ancient inns and picturesque churches take the place of the Druid's grove and the Roman camp, but the permanent character and widespread area of the "remains" bear witness to the favour accorded this pleasant land by the ancient Briton and his warlike conqueror, the Roman.

Up and down the Wiltshire downs, if tradition be true, our fur-clothed ancestors wended their way to mysterious rites at Stonehenge and Avebury; later on the Roman Legions cut their roads straight as an arrow o'er hill and dale, built cities in the Cotswold vales, and left remnants of villas replete with all those accessories of civilization in the shape of an ample water supply, a perfect bath and hypocaust, which we in these later days can only imitate.

It may be unable to boast the scenery of the Highlands or the Lake District. It may have nothing equal to the streams and mountains of North Wales, but it has a quiet charm all its own—a picture of English rural life, and English upland scenery, mingled with the marvellous and inspiring handiwork of the past.

Looking back at a holiday in the Cotswolds and North Wilts, one recalls drives over rolling downs, by cool and tiny streams, the source of a noble river, which at its flood has for centuries borne the commerce of the world : through a pleasant, verdant country, dotted with old-world villages and sleepy towns ; and then forest scenes—great avenues of beech and oak, sylvan retreats bedecked with a wealth of wild flowers and shrubs. One remembers too the silvery carillon of Cirencester ; the antique windows, of wondrous design, of Fairford church, and lastly mighty monuments—weird and solitary—of a rude and prehistoric age.

The route from the north of England is *via* Cheltenham by the Midland Railway, the pioneer Company of all that embraces cheapness and comfort in English travelling ; and from London and the South by the South Western, *via* Andover.

The tourist from the North will find in

CHELTENHAM

and its leafy environs a complete justification for the title, "Garden Town of England," and not less the Borough motto, "Salubritas et Eruditio." The author of "*The Golden Decade of a Favoured Town*" says :—"Beautiful for situation is the town of Cheltenham. Lying in a slightly undulating plain at the foot of the Cotswold Hills, she is yet sufficiently withdrawn from them to command an extensive view of their picturesque outlines. Viewed from some favoured situation in her midst, such as the playground of the College, these hills appear to encompass her on three sides, or three sections of an amphitheatre ; while on the fourth, not however visible from that site, but plainly visible from the neighbourhood of Christ Church, the Malvern Hills swell up from the horizon in a graceful undulating line of beauty that defines the entire chain. The valley plain in which the town stands is very fertile, and, seen in later spring or early summer, from one of the spurs of the Cotswolds, is thick with glorious greenery and orchard blooms. So viewed, too, the town is engagingly picturesque and attractive. Not a manufacturing chimney is seen. No polluting smoke veils her graces from the spectator's eye, or defiles her when seen. Built chiefly of stone, she reclines white-robed and easeful on the green plain, and lifts into the pure sky above her nothing but church spire or scholastic tower—signs that characterise her as a place where religion, culture and refinement hold principal sway."

When George the Third was King, Cheltenham Spa claimed "Wit and Wisdom, Fashion and Folly," as pilgrims to its medicinal springs. His Majesty took his glass of water each morning ; and the same curative salts rising to-day as then were patronised by Wellington, Byron, Scott, Perceval and Fox, among all who were famous in their age.

"Other times, other manners," Pitville Spa with its pump-room, gardens, and ornamental water remains ; the fashionable crowd promenade to band music, enjoy the luxuriant stretch of greensward and shrubbery, but go to Germany, with possibly less enjoyable surroundings, for their "cure." For all this, Cheltenham has grown and improved year by year. Its Pitville and Montpelier Gardens, its Promenade, compared to "Unter den Linden" at Berlin, its scholastic establishments and convenience as a hunting centre, have tended to bring a fashionable residential population within its borders, and the same agencies draw a host of visitors at all times and seasons of the year.

For a magnificent panorama embracing the Cotswold and Malvern Hills, with the mountains of Wales to the west, one must not miss an ascent of the Pump Room Dome at Pitville. Tiring as the upward steps may be, one is amply repaid for toil and trouble. Another coign of vantage is Leckhampton Hill, to the south-west of the town ; indeed the tourist may well spend a week in the environs of Cheltenham, among an ever-changing scene of rural and architectural beauty. Each Saturday during the season a four-horse coach leaves the "Plough Hotel" for Broadway, the out-of-the-way village in the North Cotswolds, 16 miles distant, beloved of American artists as a typical English village. Again, Gloucester Cathedral is within 10 minutes' run by train, and Tewkesbury, boasting another famous Cathedral, is eight miles only from Cheltenham. Neither of these should be missed ; nor should a six-mile drive to Sudeley Castle, close to the ancient town of Winchcombe, the capital of the Saxon kingdom of Mercia. There are good hotels in Cheltenham, of which the principal are "The Queen's," "The Plough," and "The Fleece." Omnibuses run at convenient times to the Midland Station at Lansdowne, from which we depart for the "high wild hills" towards Cirencester. At one point the line of the Midland and South Western Junction Company reaches, on The Wold, an altitude of 1000 feet above the level of the sea ; and there are some very pretty bits of woodland scenery before we reach

CHEDWORTH

lying in a vale of the hills, and one of the most picturesque of the Cotswold villages. In the woods, about a mile distant from the station, the property of Lord Eldon, are the most perfect remains of a Roman villa to be found in England. Good judges of what an estate agent would call an eligible site were these Roman warriors of old. The villa, supposed to have been the residence of the Governor of the Province, faces a characteristic Cotswold glen, and is sheltered on the north, east and west, by wooded hills. An ample water supply flows from the spring into a concrete tank, which is in good preservation, and from which the baths and the whole villa were supplied. It is only some 25 years since that burrowing rodents were credited with the discovery of this more than interesting villa. They brought to the surface a few cubes of tesselated pavement, thus leading to an excavation of the site. There were baths for the servants as well as the lordly owner, who cooled himself on mosaic pavements, still in excellent preservation ; and the latter remark applies to pavements of beautiful design in the dining hall. The hypocaust, too, is well preserved, and this, together with the pavements, have been covered in by rustic buildings. A museum is attached to the cottage, built on the spot by Lord Eldon, and a very fine collection of pottery,

On Bank Holidays, extra trains were run between Swindon and Marlborough so that people could enjoy themselves in Savernake Forest. It was also a favourite place for Sunday School outings. Specials were also run to the Marlborough Mop Fair, held in the wide High Street; the platform staff at Marlborough had to count the tickets, so that they could work out how many specials would be needed to take people home to Swindon after the events. The MSW employees had an outing each year to Ryde or Portsmouth, the fare of 3s 6d including meals and the boat trip. The Cirencester works band would play on the boat.

THE TIDWORTH BRANCH

In October 1902 five trains ran each way on the Tidworth branch, with none on Sundays. By October 1905, ten trains ran up to Tidworth and eleven down, while three additional trains ran each way on Saturdays. Most trains were scheduled to take 6 min for the journey of just over 2 miles. Five up and six down trains ran on Sundays. By May 1911 the service had increased to fourteen trains each way, seven on Sundays. The 7.33 p.m. ran non-stop from Andover Junction to Tidworth, taking 17 min. By August 1914 the service had increased to fourteen up and thirteen down trains on weekdays, and six each way on Sundays. In July 1923 the last month of its separate existence, the MSW ran ten up (two were mixed) and eight down trains. The only one to run on Sundays was from Ludgershall to Tidworth for the benefit of troops returning from leave. The front portion of the Andover-Swindon train worked this, the remainder of the train being left standing at Ludgershall till the engine returned from Tidworth to take it forward; in winter, strong complaints were often made that the Swindon portion got very cold whilst waiting.

In July 1939 ten trains ran each way on the branch, and there was still the solitary up Sunday train for returning troops. By October 1947 six of the ten up trains were mixed and three of the eight down trains; journey time had increased to 7 min, and one up train ran on Sundays. If the 10.5 a.m. from Cheltenham was too late to catch the connection with the 1.6 p.m. Andover Junction to Waterloo, the 12.25 p.m. from Tidworth would be extended to Andover Junction. By September 1955 the service had diminished to three trains each way on weekdays only.

GOODS TRAFFIC

Goods traffic was developed from the north to Southampton in the same way that the passenger traffic was encouraged. An express goods service left Manchester in the evening and arrived at Southampton in time for shipment the following morning. In the reverse direction there were through booking arrangements for fruit and vegetables from the Channel Islands and French ports to Gloucester, Birmingham and Manchester. Early potatoes from the Channel Islands came in by boatloads, and J. M. Malerbi, the district traffic superintendent at Southampton in 1900, would bribe the shunters to get the MSW trains ready first.

5,871 tons were carried in 2,685 wagons in 1913. In 1914 the figures were 6,048 and 2,456 respectively, and in 1923 had risen to 9,280 and 3,000. We are told that in 1921 sixty-three special potato trains were run. In 1922 the average number of daily through wagons between the MR and LSW was 58.

Through merchandise wagons from stations north of Cheltenham to stations south of Andover Junction (inclusive) continued to increase after 1923. The greatest number of through wagons in 1922 was 218 (weeks ending 17 June and 7 October) and this was increased to a maximum of 301 (week ending 3 June) in 1923. In fact every week in 1923 showed an increase except three (one of these was Easter week), the total increase being as much as 2,325 wagons.

Cricklade had some of the finest pasture in England and dairying was the chief farming activity, with the fattening of cattle, sheep and pigs ancillary to it. In the nineteenth century some of the milk was made into cheese, but by 1920 most was sent to London by rail, 12,000 gallons a day and four to five million gallons a year. A milk train started from Cricklade at 6.50 p.m. with four loaded vans. The guard, travelling porter and station porter lifted the churns, which weighed 2¼ cwt and held 17 gallons when full, into the vans, after the farmers had rolled them up. Sixty churns were loaded at Blunsdon, twenty to twenty-five at Moredon, and another van was picked up at Rushey Platt. More vans were attached at Swindon, some empty and some loaded. Sixty churns were lifted in at Chiseldon at the height of the season, in May; another fourteen were loaded at Ogbourne. At Marlborough the train picked up some more vans, already loaded, and another one or two were added at Savernake. At Grafton another sixty churns would be lifted in, though this would drop to about forty in winter. The train, with seventeen or so loaded vans, finally arrived at Andover some time between 9 and 10 p.m.; an LSW engine and guard were ready to take them on to Clapham Junction and Waterloo.

Just before absorption, the 5 p.m. milk and passenger train which ran on Sundays between Cricklade and Andover, was one of the country's slowest: it was allowed 3 hours, less only 6 minutes, for a distance of 41 miles. It was allowed no less than 10 minutes at Blunsdon, Chiseldon and Grafton and no wonder, for on 6 March 1921, 409 churns had to be loaded on to it, bringing receipts of £47 13s 5d, the mileage proportion giving an average of 20-25 per cent of the carriage to the MSW.

In June 1923, out of a daily total of 759 churns, 299 went to Vauxhall, 148 to Clapham Junction, 111 to Waterloo, and the rest to other London stations, apart from two for Cheltenham and one for Swindon. The 1923 churn census showed an increase of 129 daily on the 1922 census. In June 1923, the greatest number of churns came from Cricklade—195 daily. Grafton was second with 146. On weekdays the crew of the milk train returned from Andover at 12.15 a.m. with the empties. Dropping these off at the stations was a noisy job. The churns had brass plates with the owner's name on and these had to be sorted out by the light of a handlamp. Sometimes the empty milk train would stop outside Marlborough Tunnel so that the crew could catch rabbits. At the following stations the driver and fireman would come back to help with unloading to make up for lost time.

A dairy was opened at Latton near Cricklade and milk went there by road in increasing quantities; the traffic was mostly lost to the railway by about 1935, though some churns were carried until the late 1940s.

The places with the heaviest 'coaching' and freight receipts totals for 1921 were: Tidworth £53,588, Swindon £40,517, Cirencester £21,300, Marlborough £17,801, Weyhill £15,572, Cricklade £14,665, and Chiseldon £12,348.

Horse traffic was important, and in 1922 one hundred racehorses were conveyed to the Doncaster meeting alone. Brood mares and polo ponies were carried from Cirencester as well as cans of seminal fluid from the stallions for artificial insemination. With increasing road transport, the railway carried less racehorse traffic and the Western Region (ex-GWR) road horseboxes for conveying animals between stations and stables in the Swindon and Marlborough areas were withdrawn on 7 June 1952.

One stopping goods ran from Cheltenham to Andover and back, carrying hay, straw, etc.; it took ten to eleven hours each way and in consequence the footplate crew were given 1s 6d lodging money, though the guards changed at Swindon and returned home. In the reverse direction the pick-up goods had to shunt at all stations except Ludgershall, Swindon Town and Cirencester, which had their own engines. It often arrived at Cheltenham with fifty to sixty wagons.

Some goods trains ran at excellent speeds. The 3 a.m. goods ex-Cheltenham High Street, pulled by an 0—6—0, arrived at Southampton 90½ miles away at 7.20 a.m. with stops at Swindon, Andover and Romsey totalling 20 minutes, giving an average speed of just over 24 m.p.h. This train was followed by the 4.45 with a running time only 10 min longer. The 9.30 p.m. up from Southampton to Cheltenham Lansdown had an average running speed of over 25 m.p.h., excellent considering that it was over a single line for a greater part of the distance.

A regular freight train service was run daily from the GWR at Westbury to Ludgershall *via* Wolfhall Junction, chiefly for traffic from the Reading and Bristol directions.

PERMANENT WAY

The Marlborough Railway was originally laid with the usual ex-broad-gauge 62 lb per yd bridge rail, fixed to longitudinal sleepers.[1] The SMA track from Rushey Platt to Marlborough was Krupps flat-bottomed steel rail, 70 lb per yd, held in wrought-iron chairs, those at the joints weighing 6¼ lb and the intermediate ones 4⅓ lb. From Wolfhall Junction to Andover Junction the permanent way was the same, except that the chairs were cast and not wrought iron. These light chairs did not secure the rail firmly enough on the outside of curves and were replaced in 1895 by special cast-iron chairs weighing 36 lb each. The flat-bottom rail had a long life; at least one length survived into the 1950s at the end of a siding at Swindon Town. Some of the Krupps rail was sold to the Wantage Tramway, with which there was some connection, as its manager, W. A. Noble, left the MSW goods manager's office in 1899 and frequently after his appointment negotiated for second-hand MSW equipment; J. Bullock also left the MSW and was appointed to the Wantage Tramway as goods manager in 1900.[2]

North of Rushey Platt the line was laid with 75 lb per yd bull-headed steel rail, held in chairs by compressed oak keys on the inside, instead of the more usual outside position. The MGR had heavier bull-headed rail weighing 87 lb per yd which became standard on the MSW from 1900-14. When the MGR was built and the existing line from Wolfhall to Grafton was doubled, the light flat-bottom rails were replaced and put into Savernake siding. When 85 and 95 lb rail was adopted as the British standard, E. Connal, the MSW's engineer, wanted to adopt the 95 lb, but was instructed to use the 85 lb, probably on the grounds of expense. By 1923 the main line was all laid with 87 lb rail, except for the down road between Andoversford and Cirencester, which had 75 lb. The Tidworth branch also had 75 lb rail.

The bottom ballast for the first four miles of the SMA from Rushey Platt was stone, and the rest chalk; top ballast was broken stone, flint and gravel. SCE ballast was similar except for one mile of burnt clay. Fencing on the SMA was post and rail, while north of Cirencester it was chiefly larch post and wire, with stone walls in a few places. Fencing on the MGR was woven wire, 11 ft 10 in. high.

SIGNALS

Originally signals were only fitted with a red spectacle glass so that a white light shone when a signal was pulled off; green was substituted for white in the 1890s. The MSW worked distant signals on single-line sections, but the GWR changed to fixed caution boards.

The Cheltenham extension was from the beginning worked by Tyer's electric tablet system which, as the result of an undertaking given the Board of Trade in 1891, replaced the staff and ticket method, with disc block telegraph, used on the older parts of the line. Sykes' lock and block was used on the double-track MGR, but as traffic did not justify this it was replaced in 1902 by Tyer's three-position single-wire block indicators, which had been used on the recently doubled MSW sections. When Rushey Platt and Wolfhall Junction signal boxes were rebuilt in 1905, Sykes locking frames were installed, and signals of the type used by the LSW were supplied by Evans, O'Donnell & Co. After its singling by the GWR, the Andoversford-Cirencester stretch used the electric train token system.

The signal lamps were put out every morning, taken to the lamp room to be cleaned, and replaced in the evening; they would only burn for eighteen hours. If the porters thought they could escape notice, they took the oil to the distant signals and filled them on the spot to avoid a double journey. A home signal at Marlborough station and the up distant at Collingbourne had a lamp on a chain, which could be lowered for filling and cleaning.

A speed limit of 15 m.p.h. was observed for changing the tablet; the brass tablets were put in rubber pouches with iron hoops (though some had rubber handles in later days) and after fast runs, firemen used to go home at the end of the day with arms bleeding from the force of the loop—enduring this for 3s 6d a day. In the later days, the black leather tablet pouch had a rope handle covered with leather; the handle became supple after use, not staying erect for the fireman to catch it. So the pouches with a stiff rope were kept for fast trains and those running after dark.

On 13 June 1927 telephone and electric token key boxes were introduced between Cirencester and Swindon for permanent-way department trolley working. This allowed mechanically-propelled trolleys to be taken off in mid-section, the restoration of the key in a lineside box enabling a token to be released in a signal box. Known as the 'economic' system of permanent-way maintenance, it allowed three gang-lengths to be worked by one gang, and £1,185 was saved annually between Cirencester and Marlborough. The 'economic' system was extended from Swindon Town 'B' to Marlborough on 25 August 1930, from Cirencester to Andoversford the same month and from Marlborough to Savernake High Level and Low Level on 2 October 1933.

The crossing loops at Ogbourne and Chiseldon were signalled for running in either direction. This arrangement, which came into operation on 8 February 1952, made it possible to switch out the boxes on Sundays and operate one long section between Swindon Town 'B' box and Marlborough.

ACCIDENTS AND MISHAPS

The MSW was mercifully free from large-scale accidents. The first fatality came in May 1881, while the SMA was being built. A navvy tipping soil at West Grafton slipped while leading a horse with a loaded wagon and was run over by the wagon wheel. And in July that year, during the period that the line was awaiting inspection and a free service was being run, a guard had his foot crushed, as mentioned in Chapter 2.

The fatal accident to J. Y. Choules, a goods guard, at Weyhill on 16 October 1891, was of more consequence in that it brought to light the absurdly long hours some of the employees would work.[3]

Choules, aged twenty-two, was crushed between two wagons while shunting; he was himself to blame, having failed to keep a look-out —but he had been on duty for 22h. 18m. consecutively.

> In the 27 days before his death, he had worked on 24, his average daily working hours being 12h. 58m., and a table given shows the following working hours in the last fortnight of his life:
>
> | October 3 | 19h. |
> |---|---|
> | 6 | 19h. 55m. |
> | 8 | 20h. |
> | 10 | 17h. 48m. |
> | 13 | 23h. 15m. |
> | 15 | 22h. 18m. |
>
> The driver of the train had been on duty at the time of the accident for 23h. 48m. but had declined relief.

Major Marindin, the inspecting officer, found that one driver was from 16-18 October on duty 47h. 40m., with only twenty minutes' rest between two turns of 25h. 40m. and 18h. From 26-29 October he was on duty for 61 hours with two intervals of 4h. 40m. and 4h. between turns of 26h., 13h. and 22h. Another driver was once on duty for 38 hours out of 41. Marindin's report, which was presented to Parliament and had useful results, concluded:

> The company have since this accident made some alterations in their timetable, which have, I am told, somewhat improved the punctuality of their trains; and something to lessen the fearfully long hours of duty might be done by a rearrangement of hours and the institution of a proper system of relieving the men when necessary, but I fear that nothing but a considerable addition to the staff will altogether remove the evil, which has become intolerable.

1895 proved to be a relatively bad year for accidents. From Andover northwards the road had been affected by frost and all drivers were warned to 'drive carefully'. On 5 April[4] the 9.15 a.m. passenger train from Andover ran off the rails at Tanner's Curve, nearly 2½ miles north of Marlborough station. The train, drawn by 2—4—0T No. 6, consisted of a new MR third-class coach, two MSW composites and an MSW brake third, all six-wheelers. The engine and the first two coaches went halfway down the 10 ft high embankment but the other two coaches remained on the ballast. The first coach had only two passengers, which was lucky as the tender buffers stove in one end. The other compartments were full of boys returning home from Marlborough College for the Easter holiday. The crew were shaken, but no passengers were hurt. Lt-Col Yorke, the inspecting officer, considered that the warning to 'drive carefully' was not adequate. A speed of 35 m.p.h. was needed to keep to the booked time at this spot, and this he thought too fast.

An odd kind of minor disaster occurred at Rushey Platt station on 26 June 1895.[5] The lurching of the 3.10 p.m. from Andover as it passed from one curve to another near the points caused a light four-wheel LSW truck it was hauling to become derailed shortly after passing through the loop points at the south end of the station. It dragged along on the ballast beside the line for a quarter of a mile, striking the projecting ends of the platform's wooden joists and knocking them out of place so that the platform collapsed down the slope of the embankment. The stationmaster, waiting to receive the tablet for the rear section, fell with the platform and was thrown down the embankment but only bruised. The signalman, further along the 150 yd platform, ready to give the tablet for the section ahead, saved himself by running down the bank at the north end of the station. The accident was caused by excessive speed.

Ogbourne was the scene of an accident on 30 April 1900.[6] 0—6—0T No. 2 had worked the 3.15 p.m. Swindon to Ogbourne market train, which consisted of two coaches and a goods brake van. The engine had run round the train on arrival at Ogbourne, and had coupled up to the brake, preparatory to taking it to the other end of the train. The chain between the van and the coaches was tight and the engine was buffered up to ease it. The impact set the coaches moving. Efforts to stop them were unavailing, and meanwhile the 2.2 p.m. up train from Southampton was approaching. Its driver did not see the porter's signals until he was only 50 yd away; the train was going at 15 m.p.h. and the runaway coaches at a good walking speed when they struck each other. The engine had its chimney knocked off, the buffer beam smashed and the smokebox door and brake gear damaged. One of the empty coaches had three compartments stove in; three passengers were injured in the up train.

Lt-Col Yorke said he thought the use of a goods brake van not fitted with a vacuum brake was contrary to the Order made by the Board of Trade on the company under the provisions of the Regulation of Railways Act 1889—as it resulted in the vacuum brake not being continuous throughout the passenger train. The company explained that it was short of rolling stock and no passenger brake van was available at Swindon for the train.

Unlike the staffs on the bigger railways, the MSW men did sometimes break rules to achieve smarter working: after all, they had it impressed on them that trains must be punctual. A wagon with a broken drawbar would be coupled on behind a brake van (with a red lamp hanging dutifully on the back of the truck) rather than left behind. Fly shunting was readily used.

What will probably prove to be the last mishap on the line occurred on 1 May 1964. The special school train bringing 400 Marlborough College boys from Paddington had arrived at Marlborough and as the Hymek diesel was running round the train, it ran off the end of the rails. Unknown to the driver, some of the track had been lifted eight weeks previously. Six hundred gallons of fuel were spilt and railwaymen from Reading worked through the night to re-rail this, the first diesel to visit the the station.

CHAPTER 10

Locomotives & Rolling Stock

MOTIVE POWER : SMA AND MSW

For the opening of the SMA, three small 0—6—0 tank engines were bought for £1,600 each. Of Dübs' standard design and really meant for goods traffic, they had large copper-capped chimneys, tall domes and long side tanks reaching to the back of the smokebox. The coal bunker was inside the cab. With 4 ft driving wheels and outside cylinders 15½ by 22 in., at first they were only fitted with a handbrake, but later Gresham & Craven's vacuum brake was added. After the company acquired passenger engines, these tanks were used principally on goods trains and transfer work on the twice-daily trips between Swindon Town and the transfer sidings east of Swindon Junction. No. 1 was stabled at Cirencester and had 'Ciren' in brass letters on its side. These three engines are said to have been rebuilt by the Avonside Engine Co. in 1900, but were probably only repaired there and had different chimneys fitted.

With the development of through traffic, larger engines were needed and Nos. 2 and 3 were sold to S. Pearson & Son in October 1906 for £1,200 for the two, being used on Pearson's Hull docks contract. In 1917 they became Nos. 9 and 10 of Redbourn Hill Iron & Coal Co. Ltd; and by 1937 No. 10 was scrapped and No. 9 out of use. No. 1 was placed on the duplicate list in 1905, re-numbered 30 in 1912 and stored at Cirencester, and in 1914 sent to Tidworth Camp. In 1916 it was sold to the Bute Works Supply Company for £750 and later worked for the Ministry of Munitions.

After the success of *Little Wonder* on the Festiniog Railway in 1869, Robert Fairlie and George England junior formed the Fairlie Engine & Steam Carriage Co. with the intention of taking over the Hatcham Ironworks at New Cross where *Little Wonder* was built. George England senior retired, and soon afterwards his son died and the works were sold in 1872. Fairlie abandoned the idea of engine building himself, and under the title of the Fairlie Engine & Rolling Stock Co. opened an office in Westminster, where from

1872 to 1878 he designed locomotives for construction by other firms.

In September 1881 Fairlie offered an 0—4—4T to the SMA and the board resolved 'that he be requested to lend to the Company the engine for trial at the Company's expense'. This engine had been built by the Avonside Engine Co. in 1878 for Fairlie's company and shown at the Paris Exhibition the same year. However, R. A. S. Abbott suggests[1] that R. & W. Hawthorn & Co.'s locomotive works No. 1699 of 1877 was built to exactly the same drawings as the one lent to the SMA, and—as there are no official records of what happened to the Hawthorn—the SMA's may have been built by Hawthorn's, not by Avonside. At first glance it looked ordinary enough, but closer inspection showed that the driving wheels were not fixed to the frames, but were on a bogie and set far forward. The cylinders were also set well forward and the front half projected beyond the line of the smokebox. Setting the trend, the steam chests were above the cylinders, and it was one of the first engines in the country to be fitted with Walschaert's valve gear— and one of the earliest tank engines to have a water tank under the coal bunker, in addition to side tanks. The trailing bogie had largish wheels, 4 ft diameter. It bore a plate 'Fairlie's Patent' on the tank sides.

The single-boiler Fairlie had the advantage of a greater tractive effort than an ordinary engine of the same weight and cylinder capacity; fixing the driving wheels on a bogie reduced friction and allowed curves to be negotiated more easily. In an experiment in the United States during the 1870s, a Fairlie hauled five to seven American cars on the Boston River Beach & Lynn Railway, whereas an ordinary American engine could only haul four.[2] After considering a report made by the traffic manager on 17 March 1882 regarding the trial of the engine on the SMA, and the cost of additions and alterations required, the company offered to buy it for £1,000. Fairlie accepted, and after he had received the cheque sent in a £30 bill for the carriage of the locomotive from Cardiff to Swindon.[3]

In January 1883 the traffic manager reported to the board that the steampipe was constantly giving way. Fairlie proposed a modification and offered to bear half the cost of alteration, a gesture readily accepted. The work was carried out in March at a cost of £60. But in 1884 the locomotive foreman reported: 'No 4 is little or no use to us for train work, as she can never be depended on and is the most expensive engine we have for working.' It burnt

45 to 50 lb of coal per mile, a heavy consumption for trains of five or six four-wheeled coaches and too heavy for the slender finances of the SMA. Possibly the locomotive foreman at Swindon did not fully understand the valve gear; with a probable leakage in the steampipe connections, the tractive effort was likely to have been far less than the nominal 10,115 lb. A. McDonnell, engineer of the Great Southern & Western, who built a similar engine at Inchicore in 1869, found that the coal consumption was 3-4 lb per mile less than the average. 'The engines work very freely, run very steadily and are very handy. They have given no trouble, except a little with the steampipes, which I made at first without any joints, but altered since.'[4]

So the SMA kept No. 4 for reserve use only. It acquired the nickname 'Jumbo', and was certainly a white elephant. In 1888 it worked for a few weeks, taking wagons between Swindon Town and Swindon transfer sidings, and then rested again. It was involved in an accident in March 1889 which brought the recommendation that continuous brakes be fitted to passenger trains as soon as possible. Although still on the books, No. 4 was not mentioned in the list of engines in the board minute-book on 12 February 1891. When Sam Fay took over in 1892 he scrapped it, but the boiler was kept to supply steam to the company's workshops at Cirencester.

For the opening to Andover, something better was required than goods tanks and a passenger engine which could 'never be depended on'. New engines were on order, but before they were delivered, in March 1882, the LSW lent three, at a rental of £2 a day.[5] The SMA decided to buy three standard Beyer Peacock 2—4—0 tank engines, for £1,993 10s 11d[6] each, and numbered them 5, 6 and 7. These, known as 'Spinning Jennies', were similar to the locomotives built for the Dutch State Railways in 1877 and 1878 by the same builders, with polished brass domes, a tall, tapering, copper-capped chimney, a low-roofed cab—and a wooden bung to the water-filler cap. The absence of angle iron round the footplate gave a delicate appearance. Like 'Jumbo', they had 5 ft 6 in. driving wheels, but larger cylinders, 16 by 24 against 16 by 22 in. They were fitted with both steam and vacuum brake. As originally built the cab sides were narrower than the tanks. In front were two large round lookouts close together, with two rectangular windows at the back; the MSW fitted them later with wider cabs. In the early days, two were based at Swindon, one working two daily trips each way and the other working one trip each direction and part of the goods service. The other 2—4—0T worked the passenger and mixed trains on the Swindon to Cirencester service.

In June 1883 three more were ordered, but only No. 8 was delivered, at a cost of £1,925[7], as the SMA could not pay for the others; Beyer Peacock had to dispose of them elsewhere. No. 8 was similar to the first batch, though rather larger and had inside cylinders of 17 by 24 in. The wheelbase was 1 ft 6 in. longer, and E. L. Ahrons (*Locomotive and Train Working in the Latter Part of the Nineteenth Century*) considered it rode better than the others. It had outside instead of inside bearings to the leading wheels and a higher and more weatherproof cab. Its water-filler covers were the usual metal type. No. 5 was withdrawn in 1912. No. 6 was sold to the Isle of Wight Central Railway in November 1906 for £700, becoming that line's No. 7 and in due course SR No. W7, which was scrapped in 1926. MSW No. 7 was broken up by May 1910, and No. 8, which had been renumbered 29 in 1912 so that a new engine could have its number, was sold to J. F. Wake, Darlington, in January 1918. In 1887-8 LSW Beattie No. 231 worked for several months between Swindon and Andover, and an un-recorded LSW locomotive was borrowed in 1889.

The eight engines could not cope with the traffic when the extension to Cheltenham was opened and two Beattie 2—4—0 engines were borrowed, together with two train sets. When Sam Fay managed to obtain through running powers to Southampton, a larger engine was urgently needed, but unfortunately there were no funds to buy one. Percy Mortimer, one of the directors, loyally came to the rescue and personally advanced £2,360 for No. 9, a Dübs 4—4—0.[8] This engine had 6 ft driving wheels and 17 by 24 in. outside cylinders; designed by the makers, it was similar to engines they had built for the Cambrian Railways. Like all subsequent MSW engines, it had its whistle on the cab roof. It originally had a plain stovepipe chimney, but after 1899 was fitted with a parallel iron-capped one. It worked the North and South Expresses and the American and Cape mail trains too. No. 9 was withdrawn immediately after amalgamation, never carrying its GWR number.

More engines were needed for the increasing through traffic, and as mentioned earlier Sam Fay managed to get the Court of Chancery to agree to the setting up of a rolling-stock fund with a loan of £56,000. Sir Charles Scotter, general manager of the LSW, and Sir Michael Hicks-Beach, MSW director, were trustees. This paid the outstanding debts to the Metropolitan Carriage & Wagon Co. and bought:

MSW LOCOMOTIVES IN THE GWR ERA—2
(38) 'Galloping Alice' after rebuilding, 1925
(39) No. 843

MSW LOCOMOTIVES IN THE GWR ERA—3

(40) *No. 27 after rebuilding*
(41) *No. 1005 after rebuilding*

		£	s	d
6	engines	12,959	4	0
1	coach	765	0	0
15	wagons	924	0	0
7	milk vans	927	10	0
3	goods brake vans	342	15	0
3	horse boxes	491	5	0

The engines purchased were Nos. 10, 11, 12, 13, 4 (0—6—0T) and 14 (2—6—0). Nos. 10, 11 and 12 were 2—4—0 tender engines, also built by Dübs. The bogie may have been abandoned on the grounds of weight or expense. These engines were similar to No. 9 and had the same-sized cylinders, but the driving wheels were 6 in. smaller; the 27-ton tenders were standard with No. 9. At first they had stovepipe chimneys, but in 1903 No. 12 received a cast-iron one. They often worked the Saturday-morning Ocean boat-trains. They were rebuilt at Swindon in 1924 with S/11 domed boilers and sent to the Reading area.[9] The coal rails on the tender were replaced by solid coal guards. One of these 2—4—0s was used as a station pilot at Newbury and in 1927 when No. 6003 *King George IV*, pulling the Cornish Riviera Express, derailed a bogie at Theale, the ex-MSW engine took the train on to Westbury. Although on grouping they were the second-oldest engines, they outlasted the others by nearly thirteen years and were the only MSW engines to be taken over by British Railways. Nos. 10 and 11 were withdrawn in 1952 as Nos. 1334 and 1335, No. 12 (1336) lasting for two years longer and completing 506,867 miles since 1923. Stamped on the edge of the GWR cast-iron numberplates was 'Ex M&SW No.—', though this was not noticeable when covered with grime.

Nos. 13 and 4 (renumbered 14 in 1914) were bought at the same time. 0—6—0Ts, they had 4 ft 7 in. driving wheels and cylinders 17 by 24 in. Both engines were usually stationed at Swindon. They became GWR Nos. 825 and 843.

In 1895, Beyer Peacock sold to the MSW a surplus 2—6—0 which had been built for a South American railway, and was similar to engines the firm had built for New South Wales. No. 14 had bar frames, an unusually low running plate and small splashers over the 4 ft driving wheels. The horizontal cylinders were 18 by 26 in. and the piston rods tailed through the front covers. The trailing axle passed under the long firebox. The boiler was fed by one injector and one pump worked from the piston crosshead. At the time it was bought it was the only 2—6—0 in the country. The tender springs were above floor level. The roof over the small

J

cab overhung the weatherboard too much, spoiling its appearance.

The engine, stationed at Cheltenham, was so satisfactory for its job of hauling through freight trains that another (No. 16) was built in 1897 and stationed at Andover; this had a larger cab with sliding windows, but was otherwise similar. No. 16 was also a favourite for working ballast trains from Foss Cross. It could pull sixty wagons easily and sometimes was used on pigeon specials and milk trains. Nicknamed 'Galloping Alice', at Grafton it was known as 'Black Alice' on account of its habit of belching dirty smoke while climbing through the cutting there. On one occasion it pulled a sixty-two-wagon goods train from a standstill at Rushey Platt Low Level to Swindon Town in eight minutes, a distance of 1¾ miles up a gradient of 1 in 75. It was rumoured that the design of the pony truck for the GWR 43XX class engines was copied from No. 16; MSW men believed that Churchward, living at Swindon, saw how well the MSW 2—6—0s coped with heavy goods trains.

On grouping, No. 16 went to Swindon for overhaul, receiving an S/9 domed boiler. Renumbered 24, it was given a GW tender and cab, which resulted in the floor of the tender being above the running plate. The pistons were modified, no longer tailing through the front covers. It recommenced working in February 1925, taking the pick-up goods from Swindon transfer goods yard to Stoke Gifford yard until it was scrapped in July 1930. On one occasion, in the last few weeks of its life, it worked an express: again No. 6003 *King George IV* needed rescue by an ex-MSW engine—pulling the 11.45 Bristol-Paddington express, it failed at Badminton with a broken whistle stem. No. 24, working the pick-up goods, was commandeered to take the express to Swindon.[10]

No. 14 had a shorter public career, being withdrawn in 1914 and sold, minus the boiler which was used for washing-out purposes at Cheltenham, to J. F. Wake, Darlington, in January 1918; it was the only engine bought by the MSW not to be taken over by the GWR. Fitted with another boiler and cab, it worked at Cramlington Colliery, Northumberland, and later as No. 16 of Hartley Main Colliery Co., lasting until 1943. An engine identical with this one is preserved in the Argentine.

In 1895 No. 15, an 0—4—4 tank engine, was bought from Beyer Peacock. It had 5 ft 2 in. driving wheels and inside cylinders 17 by 24 in. Its side rods had an I-section and there was no angle-iron framing round the underside of the footplate. In MSW days it was stationed at Swindon and usually worked between Swindon Town and Cirencester or Marlborough. The GWR renumbered it 23 and rebuilt it in 1925 with an S/11 domed boiler. From October 1927 it worked the shuttle service between Swindon Town and Swindon Junction alone until it was withdrawn in February 1930.[11]

Two handsome Sharp Stewart 4—4—4 tank engines were bought in 1897: Nos. 17 and 18. They had 5 ft 3 in. driving wheels and inside 17 by 24 in. cylinders. These were used for the stopping passenger services, their good acceleration and fast running being ideal for this; but they did not steam well as the blast did not fill the chimney. Drivers used to put a 'jimmy', a ⅜ in. steel rod, over the blastpipe orifice to spread the exhaust cone and cause it to fill the chimney, but this increased the coal consumption by a quarter of a ton between Swindon and Cheltenham. The wheel arrangemen was suited to the reverse curves which abounded on the line. The engines had Adams patent bogies, and one driver said they used to 'ride like a cradle'. In October 1925 No. 17, as GWR No. 25, came out of the shops slightly Swindonised, but with its original boiler; the coal rail had been replaced by a plate so that coal capacity was increased. Until it was condemned in October 1927 it worked the shuttle train between Swindon Town and Swindon Junction.[12] No. 18 broke a spoke in a derailment at Savernake during the MSW regime—the spoke had a plate riveted on both sides. The GWR renumbered this engine 27 and rebuilt it with an S/10 domeless boiler early in 1925, with copper-capped chimney and polished brass safety-valve casing.[13] It was transferred to the Kidderminster area until it was scrapped in 1929.

In 1899, due to the development of goods traffic between the Midland Railway and Southampton and the increase of military traffic to Ludgershall, six express goods and passenger engines were obtained from Beyer Peacock. They had 5 ft 2½ in. driving wheels and 18 by 26 in. cylinders. The curved Beyer Peacock plate on the splashers looked like a nameplate. The engines proved successful though drivers thought them under-boilered, and four more were bought in 1902; costing £2,600 each, modifications raised their price by £13 14s 9d. They were built with large square splashers over the rear wheels, but these were altered to round ones so that the firebox was more exposed and repairs could be carried out more easily. The 1902 batch were built with curved rear splashers. The MSW later fitted Nos. 19, 22-25 and 28 with Ross pop safety valves.

The GWR rebuilt all of the engines with S/10 boilers[14] and GWR cabs; they were the only 0—6—0 engines on the Great Western to carry conical boilers until the advent of the 2251 class in 1930.

The GWR boilers gave them more steam, but the extra weight caused axlebox trouble. Pressure at first was set at 150 lb p.s.i. but later was raised to 165 lb, increasing the tractive effort to 18,900 lb. The locomotives continued to work on the MSW section and were all withdrawn between 1934 and 1938. Quite a number had their frames patched as they cracked through fast running with passenger trains. Their mileage under Great Western ownership varied between 179,124 for No. 1004 and 239,749 for No. 1005.

MIDLAND AND SOUTH WESTERN JUNCTION RAILWAY

Maximum loads of goods trains hauled by 4—4—0 and 0—6—0 tender engines

	Cirencester to Swindon (through)	Cheltenham to Swindon Tn (local)	Swindon to Ludgershall (through)	Marlborough to Ludgershall (local)	Ludgershall to Andover Jct
Heavy	16	19	19	20	28
General	26	27	27	30	40
Empties	35	35	35	40	50

	Andover Jct to Ludgershall (local)	Ludgershall to Marlborough (local)	Marlborough to Swindon Tn (local)	Swindon Tn to Cirencester (local)	Cirencester to Cheltenham (local)
Heavy	20	28	28	28	18
General	30	35	35	35	28
Empties	40	50	50	50	38

	Through Fast Goods		Loads between Andover Jct and Sou'ton and back	Swindon Tn to Rushey Platt (transfer)
	Andover to Swindon	Swindon to Cheltenham		
Heavy	30	28	30	28
General	40	35	40	35
Empties	50	50	50	50

Sketches of Great Western engines of the 'Bulldog' and 'Duke of Devonshire' types were studied in 1904, but James Tyrrell, the MSW's locomotive superintendent, disliked the heavy frames of the 'Dukes' and their inaccessibility; he designed his own 4—4—0s, which proved to be freer running than the 'Dukes'. Because of the gradients and curves the driving wheels had to be not too big, and the wheelbase not too long; the engine had also to be capable of taking a load of 300 tons up 1 in 75 banks. The design fulfilled these conditions well. The directors resolved that tenders should be invited for one engine, to be paid for out of revenue, with the option to take a second engine at the same price any time within twelve months—the option to be exercised if several of the smaller engines could be sold off. Two 0—6—0Ts and a 2—4—0T were sold in 1906, but a second 4—4—0 was not acquired until 1909.

No. 1 was built in 1905 by the North British Locomotive Company. It had 5 ft 9 in. driving wheels and inside cylinders 18 by 26 in. When new the motion was sent to Cirencester in the tender. It worked expresses and fast goods from Cheltenham and Southampton, making a double trip daily, and covered 321,740 miles before it required general repair.

In 1907 the North British offered to supply a similar engine to No. 1, which cost £2,935, for £3,525, but the MSW postponed the purchase. Prices fell and eight were built between 1909 and 1914. In 1910 No. 6 cost £2,760, No. 7 costing £2,790 in 1911. Nos. 4 and 31 had a top feed in a small dome on which the Ross pop safety valves were fitted, placed behind the steam dome. At the time, top feed was rare. After being taken over by the GWR most of these engines were fitted with an S/2 domeless boiler, the two others (Nos. 1119, 1122) being fitted with double-domed boilers. The taper boilers had a pressure of 165 lb p.s.i. giving a tractive effort of 17,120 lb, but about 1930 pressure was raised to 180 lb, increasing the tractive effort to 18,680 lb. Some of the old MSW boilers were fitted with GWR superheaters. No. 1119 acquired 1128's double-domed boiler in December 1924 after the latter had been rebuilt, but was fitted with an older boiler in March 1932. The reboilered engines were converted to right-hand drive; the 0—6—0s were right-hand drive already. The engines were withdrawn between 1931 and 1938, No. 1120 having covered 167,518 miles and No. 1126 345,095 miles.

In the last twenty-four years of its existence, the MSW standardised on 4—4—0s and 0—6—0s as did its associate, the Midland Railway. On absorption the company owned twenty-nine locomotives: ten 4—4—0, ten 0—6—0, three 2—4—0, one 2—6—0, two 4—4—4T, two 0—6—0T, one 0—4—4T. In April 1922 the engines were allotted to sheds as follows: Cheltenham, fourteen (seven spare); Cirencester, one; Swindon Town, six; Andover Junction, five. Three engines were in the shops for repairs.

GWR No.	MSW No.	Date built	S/2 boiler	Withdrawn
1119	1	7/05	★	5/35
1120	2	4/09	2/28	8/31
1121	3	4/09	9/24	3/36
1122	4	6/14	★	11/35
1123	5	4/12	8/29★	4/38
1124	6	4/10	1/26	8/35
1125	7	2/11	★	2/32
1126	8	4/12	11/28★	12/38
1127	31	6/14	10/24	10/35

★ Denotes MSW superheated boiler: 1119, 12/24; 1122, 10/30; 1123, 2/26 to 1929; 1125, 10/24; 1126, 10/25 to 1928

THE POST-MSW LOCOMOTIVES

'Dukes' assisted the MSW 4—4—0s with the through trains, and small GWR tanks on a running-in turn worked the shuttle service between Swindon Town and Swindon Junction when the MSW engines were at the works for heavy repairs or rebuilding. Cambrian Railways 0—6—0s Nos. 849, 855 and 875 appeared. After 1930 the Swindon Town—Junction shuttle service was a running-in turn for Great Western engines, and 55XX engines were used if nothing was suitable ex-works, though 2—4—0T No. 1498 and double-frame 0—6—0T No. 1620 were popular engines for the turn. The shuttle train earned the title of 'Old Town Bunk'; it was run entirely for the convenience of long-distance passengers as the rail distance was 3½ miles as opposed to 1½ miles by tram, the latter being cheaper. The train was a great favourite of locomotive spotters, many of whom travelled on it with privilege tickets, to see new engines outside the works.

'Dukes' working regularly on the MSW section were: 3258 *The Lizard*, 3260 *Mount Edgcumbe*, 3261 *St Germans*, 3264 *Trevithick*, 3269 *Dartmoor*, 3284 *Isle of Jersey*, 3289 (unnamed) and 3290 *Severn*. As 'Dukes' were the largest engines allowed on the MSW, several were transferred from the Central Wales Division for Tidworth Tattoo Week. For the works' annual holiday, 20,000 passengers left the works sidings at Swindon between late on Thursday evening and early Friday morning, when the regular services started. Two trains ran to Southsea *via* the MSW, and these consisted of LSW stock pulled by a T9 which always ran tender first with empty stock, even though it could be turned at Swindon.

MAXIMUM LOADS IN THE GWR ERA

		Tons
2—6—0	43XX	320
4—4—0	33XX	252
4—4—0	3252	
0—6—0	2251	196
0—6—0	1003-13	
4—4—0	1119-28	152
2—4—0	1334-6	130

Above maximum loads were permitted for special troop trains worked by 43XX and 78XX type engines. They were allowed to take 380 tons between Cheltenham and Southampton Terminus *via* Savernake (High Level), but were restricted to 352 tons if unassisted from Cheltenham to Andoversford, or if it was necessary to run *via* Savernake (Low Level). The speed of trains between Lansdown Junction and Andoversford Junction was not allowed to exceed 40 m.p.h. and was restricted between Andoversford Junction and Andover Junction over the single and double lines to 50 m.p.h. 'Blue' group engines were restricted to 30 m.p.h. over certain bridges between Withington and Wolfhall Junction.

The GWR wanted to work the line with heavier engines (a measure which had been allowed during the first world war), so from 1930 onwards bridges were strengthened and larger GWR engines in the 'blue' classification took over traffic; all the MSW engines, except the 2—4—0s, were scrapped by 1938. 'Bulldogs' superseded the MSW 4—4—0s, and 43XX 'Moguls' replaced the MSW 0—6—0 goods engines. In 1936 the 'Dukedogs' made their trials on the line and the taper-boiler 0—6—0s and 51XX 2—6—2Ts appeared. Between 1936 and 1943 'Aberdare' 2—6—0s Nos. 2639/56/79 worked the daily goods between Gloucester and Swindon Town. No. 3279 *Tor Bay* and 3278 *Trefusis* were shedded at Andover for some years prior to their withdrawal in October and December 1938. In 1938-9, rebuilds 3210/11/23 arrived, but did not stay long as the wartime traffic made demands too heavy for them. About 1941 'Manors' appeared: No. 7808 *Cookham Manor* was probably the first and, twenty years later in 1961, it was certainly the last to work on the line.

During the second world war, 28XX engines worked freight trains and 'Moguls' were frequently used in pairs. USA-built, MoS, and

LMS 2—8—0s also appeared. In 1941, 3452 *Penguin* and 3363 *Alfred Baldwin* were hauling eight and nine-coach trains. The first 'Castle' here was No. 5085 *Evesham Abbey* which in October 1941 carried royalty to Swindon Town. 93XX engines were also seen during the war, although being heavier than their 43XX relations they were classified 'red' instead of 'blue' and should not really have been used. After the war, 'Moguls' and 'Manors' worked most of the traffic.

During part of the British Railways era, SR 'N' and 'U' class 2—6—0s worked through from Southampton to Cheltenham instead of WR engines of the same wheel arrangement. These SR engines steamed well and if required could pull heavy loads, but most of those working over the MSW section were rough riding; between Foss Cross and Cirencester, the crew often had to seek refuge on the tender. 'West Country' Pacifics were permitted to run over the line, but only did so on specials, for instance on an ambulance train in 1945. On one occasion when a regular engine broke down at Cheltenham, a 41XX 2—6—2T worked through to Andover. BR standard 2—6—0 4MTs and pannier-tank engines also made their appearances.

LIVERY

The SMA engines were painted red and had the company's initials and the number painted on the tank sides. In the MSW days, the locomotive stock was painted a dark red lined out with black bands with yellow lines on either side. The buffer beams were painted vermilion edged with black, a yellow line separating the two colours. The cab interiors were painted a light yellow-brown. The number plates of the 2—4—0s, 4—4—0s and later 0—6—0Ts were polished brass with raised numbers on a vermilion ground. Nos. 14-16 and the 0—6—0s had separate raised brass figures. The lettering on the tender or tank sides was gold, shaded with blue. Lettering was 'M. & S.W.J. Ry' and later 'M.S.W J.R.' (or Ry). The 4—4—0s had red wheels, and those coming out in 1914 had the company's initials on the tender in gilt script instead of block lettering; this was adopted as standard—the man who designed it was given £5. Goods engines were painted an olive green though the 0—6—0s did not revert to this after the war. During the war many engines were painted unlined black, passenger engines being black lined in vermilion.

MSW engines had the old square-section lamp brackets, like the LNW; the idea was to prevent the locomotive and carriage depart-

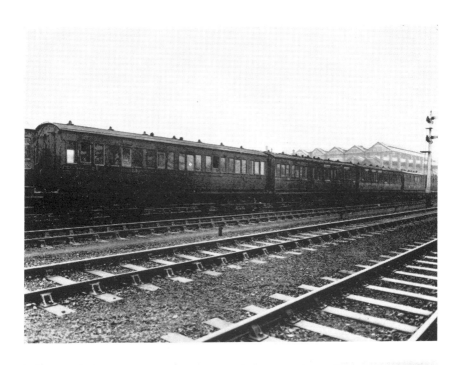

TOWN AND COUNTRY

(42) *Condemned* MSW *coaches at Swindon Works*
(43) *'Duke' class No. 3278 'Trefusis' approaching Chiseldon on down
passenger train, August 1935*

TIDWORTH BRANCH

(44) 80096 *shunting at Ludgershall*
(45) *Tidworth from buffers, c.* 1906

LOCOMOTIVES IN THE BR ERA—1

(46) *76028 leaving Collingbourne Kingston Halt with Southampton train,*
April 1961

(47) *Works holiday special, Swindon to Portsmouth, leaving*
Marlborough drawn by No. 6327, July 1961

LOCOMOTIVES IN THE BR ERA—2

(48) *No. 6395 with the 5.45 p.m. Swindon Junction—Andover, the last down train, leaving Swindon Town, September 1961*

(49) *D7044 on the down road at Swindon Town, April 1965*

ments purloining each other's lamps as the fittings were different.

MAINTENANCE

The MSW decided to save the expense of sending engines to Nine Elms for repair by building its own repair depot. In January 1895 plans of land available at Swindon and Cirencester for the proposed workshops were inspected, and as the Swindon site was insufficient, Cirencester was chosen. The cost of the workshops and machinery was estimated to be £2,000, paid out of the rolling-stock fund, as described earlier in the chapter. Work was started straight away and the shops opened later that year. The principal buildings were the machinery-fitting shop, the carriage and wagon shop, the gas-production plant, smiths' shop, wagon-repair shed, paint shop and stores. A 25-ton overhead travelling crane was provided. The engine-fitting shop was enlarged in 1903 and the works further enlarged in 1915, extending the area of the buildings to 3,947 sq yd. Four locomotives could be taken at a time.

About seventy-five men were employed at the works at the turn of the century. Work began at 6 a.m. and was hard, but the works had its own social life: the works football team paid £13 a year rent for a field and pavilion, and there was also a works band, which played on the annual outing, already described.

The fitters, painters and skilled men were moved from Cirencester in 1924, but the buildings were not finally closed until 26 October 1925. The employees were transferred to Swindon, each paying 13s for a special season ticket lasting for six months; the GWR agreed to run a train between Cirencester and Swindon for ex-MSW workmen as long as there were three requiring it—the train acquired the name of 'Stephenson'. At present the Cirencester premises belong to a scrap-metal merchant and are piled high with redundant road vehicles.

PASSENGER ROLLING STOCK

In 1881 the SMA bought ten new composite carriages from the Metropolitan Carriage & Wagon Company, Birmingham. They made a very good impression, the *Swindon Advertiser*[15] saying 'They are of light and graceful appearance, and are remarkably roomy and comfortable.' The *Marlborough Times*[16] too thought that the carriages 'are capacious and apparently well fitted up, the jolting inseparable from a newly-made line being reduced to a minimum by means of that panacea, india-rubber'. However, some of the third-class compartments had only plain wooden seats. A small destination board was on the roof in the centre of each coach.

In 1882 the company needed more stock for the opening of the extensions. The Metropolitan Carriage & Wagon Co. sent a letter[17] dated 17 March offering the following terms for purchase over seven years—as the company could not afford the outlay all at once.

> Three third-class carriages with 6 compartments each 5 ft 5 in. long in the clear—£69 10s per annum. Four third-class brake carriages, brake compartment 10 ft 11 in. long in centre and two third-class compartments each 5 ft 5 in. long at each end—£66 12s per annum. (In this type of coach, the roof swept down over the guard's look-out. These were later converted to milk and parcels vans.) Three first and second-class composites with two first-class compartments each 7 ft long and three second-class compartments 6 ft long—£80 16s per annum. Two second-class and third-class composites with three second-class compartments 6 ft long and three third-class compartments 5 ft 5 in. long —£74 12s per annum.

The only brake power was in the guard's van and wooden brake blocks pressed on the wheels.

On delivery of these coaches, the SMA's total stock was twenty-four four- and six-wheel coaches. In October 1882, sanction was given to buy forty footwarmers at not more than 13s 9d each for use in the coaches; in the following January the traffic manager asked for a house and boiler for heating the footwarmers, but it was resolved 'that as the winter had so far advanced, the matter should stand over'. When at last they were available[18], chilly passengers told the guard and a footwarmer awaited them at the next station.

There was of course a further shortage of rolling stock when the through service from Swindon Junction to Andover was started, and the first train consisted of LSW coaches. Most of the coaches the SMA already had were not paid for and, as recorded in Chapter 3, the builders threatened in April 1885 to resume possession; Shopland had to return all stock except the £7,500-worth already paid for.

In 1887 the railway thought of fitting vacuum brakes to the coaches and four passenger engines if the terms were reasonable, but apparently to the company's way of thinking they were not; and even two years later, after the accident to 'Jumbo', nothing was done; but in 1891 an undertaking was given to the Board of Trade that all coaches would be fitted with continuous automatic brakes. Money for this had to be borrowed from the LSW. Before these brakes were fitted, to work the communication cord passengers had to drop the window-light, lean out and pull a cord which rang a bell in the guard's van. Carriage lighting was also overhauled; the lamps were in bad repair and insufficient in number, it was reported in October 1892, trains having to be run without enough to light all the coaches. The necessary £25 had to be coaxed from the Receiver.

In preparation for the Cheltenham opening, the directors artfully arranged with the LSW and MR to run through coaches, so that the purchase of additional rolling stock could be avoided. But in 1896 two composites at £610 each, three thirds at £475 each, and one third at £481 were ordered from the Oldbury Carriage Co. The money came from the capital account of the Marlborough & Grafton Railway, so the coaches were technically its property.

The general manager was authorised on 25 November 1909 to buy ten coaches from the Midland Railway for £1,600 and, these proving satisfactory, the following year he was allowed to purchase up to ten more at the same price. Five more coaches were bought from the same source, for £165 each on rail at Derby, in 1911.

By this time, the MSW had a good stock of smooth-riding non-corridor coaches, mostly 42 ft long and fitted with steam heating and Stone's electric lighting. It was generally rumoured that Stone's fitted electric light in brake composite No. 26 free of charge as an advertisement, and that this coach ran between Cheltenham and Waterloo, but this was never confirmed.

The gas-lit coaches lacked pilot lights so that porters had to walk along the roofs and light up with a methylated-spirit torch. Paraffin torches were banned as they discoloured the mantles. Carriage cleaning was usually performed at Cheltenham, but one train was cleaned at Swindon and the LSW was paid for cleaning one at Southampton and sweeping out certain others at Andover and Southampton. Carriage and wagon examiners were stationed at Cheltenham, Cirencester and Swindon. GWR coach No. 4496 (MSW No. 41), a third, was the last MSW coach to be scrapped, being broken up about 1936.

PASSENGER-STOCK LIVERY

From 1881-96 the coach livery was brown and cream, with gold letters shaded with blue. At one period, however, the coaches were in a very bad state as the company could not afford to repaint them. In 1896 a slightly darker lake than the MR shade was adopted. The panels had a black surround with a gold stripe and vermilion line. Lettering was in gold with black shading, though the older carriages were lined with yellow in place of gold and lettered in yellow with red shading. The ends of the coaches were red and the roofs black. In 1914 the coaches were painted crimson lake with black ends and white roofs. During the war the lake was picked out with a straw colour and vermilion. The coaches were lettered SM & AR, M & SWJC Ry or Midland & South Western Junction, according to the period. The painters mixed their own shades. The old surface was burnt off and a lead colour put on. Four coats of filling were then applied and a coat of venetian red which was rubbed down with bricks. Another coat was put on, then purple-brown and two coats of lake. The panelling was chalked out and painted in and finally three coats of varnish applied. The coaches had a general painting every nine years, but every two years were returned to the shops for washing and touching up.

GOODS STOCK

Two goods brake vans ordered from the Metropolitan Carriage Company in 1881 at a cost of £130 each were probably one of the SMA's earliest rolling-stock purchases.[19]

With increasing traffic the shortage of wagons was of course acute. On 27 February 1883, twenty-five 8-ton open wagons were ordered from the Gloucester Wagon Co., at a cost of £54 net cash each or deferred payment extending over five years at £12 12s per wagon per year, or over seven years at £9 10s.[20] On 20 November 1884 the general manager accepted a proposal from the Midland Wagon Co. Ltd for the hire of ten open wagons at the rate of £5 10s per wagon annually.[21] The MSW owned some 10-ton four-wheel trolley wagons. Early wagons had wooden buffers bound near the end with iron. The guards had their own brake vans which they painted themselves inside, even hanging curtains at the small windows. As the van doors did not lock, at night the men would take their shunting poles home with them.

In 1924 some wagons were built at Derby specially for the conveyance of Burton beer; two tanks were built into an ordinary box van. During the GWR era, a Cambrian Railways six-wheel brake van was used on the MSW section.

The railway carried much horse traffic, and right at the start the SMA needed four horseboxes. As these cost £190 each and the capital outlay was not wanted, an offer from the Metropolitan Carriage Co. to supply them on seven years' deferred purchase at £35 per annum each was accepted.

In the early days the lights in the grooms' compartments burnt colza or rape oil, but in the MSW's latter period even the horseboxes had electric light. On amalgamation, however, the GWR removed the electrical equipment and fitted gas, for standardisation with its own stock.

The livery of the goods stock was light grey with white lettering, either SM & AR or M & SWJC Ry, depending on the period. The painter, paid a flat rate of 3d a letter, of course made his money on the small ones giving tare, etc.

MIDLAND AND SOUTH WESTERN JUNCTION RAILWAY.

Cashier's Office, Swindon.

17th May 1902

Received———————— Pounds *Twelve* ———— Shillings

and *nine* ————Pence, on Account of Traffic Receipts at your Station, for

16th day of *May 1902*

To Mr. *Tucker*

Chedworth Station

C. *12/9*

£ ~ " 12 " 9   ₡:

Cashier

Traffic account receipt signed by E. T. Lawrence

References

Notes to Chapter 1 (page 11)

1. *Journal* of the Royal Agricultural Society of England, 1844, p.164.
2. Gloucestershire Records Office, Q/RUM 210.
3. Ibid., Q/RUM 125.
4. 6 December 1845.
5. Southcot Jc-Basingstoke opened (broad gauge) 1 November 1848, (mixed gauge) 22 December 1856.
6. H. G. Lewin, *The Railway Mania and its Aftermath*, 1936.
7. Wiltshire Record Office, No. 78.
8. Ibid., No. 80.
9. 21 & 22 Vic. c. 82.

Notes to Chapter 2 (page 17)

1. *North Wilts Herald*, 31 July 1875.
2. Ibid., 31 July 1875.
3. 36 & 37 Vic. c. 194.
4. 7 July 1873.
5. Called Red Post(s) at least as early as 1879.
6. *Marlborough Times*, 31 July 1875.
7. *North Wilts Herald*, 31 July 1875.
8. *Swindon Advertiser*, 2 August 1875.
9. Ibid. 2 August 1875.
10. *Wilts & Gloucestershire Standard*, 14 October 1876.
11. 41 & 42 Vic. c. 13.
12. 42 & 43 Vic. c. 91.
13. SMA Minute Book.
14. Document in British Railways Board Historical Relics.
15. 16 July 1881.
16. Public Record Office, MT 29/42, p.207.
17. Ibid.
18. *The Chiseldonian*, June 1964.
19. *Swindon Advertiser*, 30 July 1881.
20. SMA Minute Book.
21. P.R.O., MT 29/43, p.90.
22. Marlborough Railway Minute Book, 8 April 1882.
23. Ibid.
24. Ibid.
25. Line from Abbotts Ann—Andover leased to the SMA at 5 per cent p.a. on the cost of works, £23,141.
26. 10 February 1883.

Notes to Chapter 3 (page 32)

1. 44 & 45 Vic. c. cxlvi.
2. SCE Minute Book.
3. Working agreement dated 10 June 1883.
4. Inspected by Col Rich 6 September and re-inspected 11 October 1882.
5. 46 & 47 Vic. c. cxx.
6. SCE Minute Book.
7. Ibid.
8. 47 & 48 Vic. c. lxiv.
9. 47 & 48 Vic. c. lxviii.
10. 50 Vic., Sess. 2, c. xlii.
11. MSW Minute Book.
12. 25 April 1891, p.491.

Notes to Chapter 4 (page 47)

1. 27 October 1883, Marlborough Railway Minute Book.
2. Ibid.
3. Wiltshire Records Office, 142.
4. Marlborough Railway Minute Book.
5. Ibid.
6. 59 & 60 Vic. c. ccxxx.
7. *Marlborough Times*, 14 May 1898.
8. Ibid., 18 June 1898.
9. Ibid., 2 July 1898.
10. 62 & 63 Vic. c. clxxviii.
11. 22 February 1896.
12. *Railway Times*, 8 April 1899, p.459.
13. Ibid., 24 June 1899, p.799.
14. 10 April 1899, scheduled to MR Act of 1899.
15. 1,350 tons of rails required, 65 tons of fishplates, 250 tons of chairs.
16. 400 tons of rails required 20 tons of fishplates, 250 tons of chairs.
17. Cowan & Sheldon, 55 ft cost £536, wood for engine shed £280.
18. Inspected 24 July and opened 28 July 1902.
19. *GWR Magazine*, Vol. 35, p.493.
20. BR Records, MSW 4/1.
21. *Railway Times*, 31 January 1903, p.14.

Notes to Chapter 5 (page 71)

1. *Railway Magazine*, 1950, p.501.
2. E. S. Tonks (editor), *Industrial Locomotives of Southern England*, 1958. (Birmingham Locomotive Club.)
3. Three sets of double gates, and the rest single gates between fields.

Notes to Chapter 6 (page 77)

1. Opened 1792.
2. C. F. D. Marshall and R. W. Kidner, *A History of the Southern Railway*, 1963.
3. C. Hadfield, *Canals of Southern England*, 1955.

4. 21 & 22 Vic. c. lxxxii.
5. 23 & 24 Vic. c. l.
6. 25 & 26 Vic. c. clxxvii.
7. Contractor claimed for payment of £22,000.
8. 26 & 27 Vic. c. cix.
9. *Railway Magazine*, 1910, p.52.
10. 24 & 25 Vic. c. clxvii.
11. *Marlborough Times*, 2 April 1864.
12. Glos. Records Office, Q/RUM 287.
13. Ibid., Q/RUM 307.
14. *Wilts & Glos. Standard*, 28 May 1881.
15. Glos. Records Office, Q/RUM 390.
16. P.R.O., MT 29/42.59.

Notes to Chapter 7 (page 83)

1. With effect from 1 July 1923. Davies, general manager of the MSW, retired, on 28 September.
2. 25 January 1929.
3. *North Wilts Herald*, 28 March 1929.
4. 1 December 1930.
5. 1 April 1932.
6. 28 September 1924 (passengers).
7. 1 April 1927.
8. 1 October 1932.
9. *Railway Magazine*, 1960, p.889.
10. Officially sidings from 14 June 1965.

Notes to Chapter 8 (page 92)

1. *GWR Magazine*, July 1940.
2. Savernake, renamed Savernake Low Level 1 July 1924.
3. *Marlborough Times*, 15 September 1961.
4. Building demolished 1964.
5. *Railway Magazine*, 1960, p.889.
6. Called Dowdeswell until 1 October 1892.
7. E. S. Tonks (editor), *Industrial Locomotives of Southern England*.

Notes to Chapter 9 (page 108)

1. P.R.O., MT 29/25, p.157.
2. S. H. Pearce Higgins, *Wantage Tramway*, 1958.
3. *Railway Times*, 23 April 1892.
4. *General Report to the Board of Trade on Accidents*, 1895.
5. Ibid.
6. *General Report to the Board of Trade on Accidents*, 1900.

Notes to Chapter 10 (page 125)

1. *The Engineer*, 1960, p.424.
2. BRB Archives, LIB 5/18.
3. SMA Minute Book.

K

4. BRB Archives, LIB 5/16.
5. SMA Minute Book.
6. SMA Minute Book.
7. Ibid.
8. MSW Minute Book.
9. E. R. Mountford, *Railway Observer*, 1962, pp.6, 62.
10. K. J. Cook, *Railway Observer*, 1962, p.95.
11. E. R. Mountford, *Railway Observer*, 1962, pp.6, 62.
12. Ibid.
13. Ibid.
14. Ibid.
15. 30 July 1881.
16. 2 July 1881.
17. SMA Minute Book.
18. Ibid.
19. SMA Minute Book.
20. Ibid.
21. Minutes of Permanent Way & General Purposes Committee, SMA.

Appendices

1: LOCAL AND PERSONAL ACTS
2: AGREEMENTS
3: MILEAGES
4: STATIONS AND HALTS
5: MSW LOCOMOTIVES

1 : LOCAL AND PERSONAL ACTS

1. SMA, incorporation of company; construction of railway, 36-7 Vic. c. cxciv. Extension of time for works; abandonment of parts, further powers &c, 41-2 Vic. c. xiii; 42-3, Vic. c. xci; 43-4 Vic. c. xviii; 45-6 Vic. c. cxcv; 46-7 Vic. c. cxxi. Amalgamation with SCE, 47-8 Vic. c. lxiv.

2. SCE, incorporation of company; construction of railway, 44-5 Vic. c. cxlvi. Further powers, 46-7 Vic. c. vii; 46-7 Vic. c. cxx; 47-8 Vic. c. lxviii.

3. Midland & South Western Junction Railway, formation of company by amalgamation of SMA and SCE, 47-8 Vic. c. lxiv. Further powers, 50 Vic. c. xlvi; 50-1 Vic. c. xlii; 62-3 Vic. c. clxxviii. Abandonment of railway, 52-3 Vic. c. clxiii. Rates and charges for merchandise traffic, 55-6 Vic. c. lii. Conversion and consolidation of debenture stocks; additional 'C' debenture stock, 60-1 Vic. c. cxxviii; 62-3 Vic. c. clxxviii. Agreement with the Midland Company, 62-3 Vic. c. cvii; 2 Ed. VII c. cli; 2-3 Geo. V c. lxxxi. Company and subsidiary undertakings merged with Western Group of amalgamated railways as GWR, 11-2 Geo. V c. 55, Sch. 1. Absorbed with GW Western Group Railways Scheme, SR & O, 1923, No. 1221. Undertaking vested in British Transport Commission through acquisition of GWR by Commission 10-11 Geo. VI c. 49, Sch. 3 Pt. 1.

4. Cheltenham Station Act, 53-4 Vic. c. ccxii.

5. MGR, incorporation of company; construction of railway, 59-60 Vic. c. ccxxx. Acquired by MSW, 62-3 Vic. c. clxxviii.

6. South Hampshire Railway & Pier, incorporation of company; transfer of Southern Section of MSWR, 49-50 Vic. c. cxvi. Further powers, extension of time, 52-3 Vic. c. cxcviii; 54-5 Vic. c. cxxxi.

2 : AGREEMENTS

Between	Subject	Date
MR and MSW	Access to Cheltenham	14.1.90
„	Use of Cheltenham passr & goods stations	10.6.95
„	Loan of £200,000	10.4.99
„	Loan of £50,000	30.6.02
„	Ranking of interest on loans	27.2.12
„	Exchange of land at Cheltenham	30.3.16
MSW, MR and GWR	Improved facilities between Andoversford and Cheltenham	14.3.99
MSW, Banbury & Cheltenham and GWR	Conditions of user of Banbury & Cheltenham Railway	16.5.91
SCE and GWR	Grant to use and maintain two bridges	10.12.86
MSW and GWR	Running powers to Ludgershall etc	30.4.03
GWR and MSW	Erection of telephone wires for MSW between Lansdown and Andoversford Jc.	29.10.17
SMA and LSW	Andover Jc. station and Red Post line	21.7.73
„	Running powers to Southampton	28.6.82
„	Running powers to Southampton	15.8.82
MSW and LSW	Use of Andover Jc. station and Red Post line	29.10.87
LSW and MSW	Additional works at Red Post	1.6.17
Promoters of Cheltenham Station Co. and MSW	Provision and user of a station at Cheltenham	10.4.90
Cheltenham Station Co., MSW and MR	Agreement for transfer of undertaking of Cheltenham Station Co.	10.6.95
HM Principal Secretary of State for the War Dept and MSW	Construction of Ludgershall & Tidworth Railway	19.11.99
„	Working of Ludgershall & Tidworth Railway	16.2.03
„	Haulage of traffic at Tidworth	31.8.12

In addition there were 106 minor agreements relating to private sidings, cartage agencies, tenancies, etc.

3 : MILEAGES

	Via MGR		Original route via Sav. L.L.		Distance from Red Post Jc.	
	M	C	M	C	M	C
Southampton	—	—				
Southampton Central	1	41				
Redbridge	4	25				
Romsey	9	58				
Kimbridge Jc.	12	58				
Stockbridge	19	25				
Andover Jc.	27	69				
Red Post Jc.	29	34			—	—
Weyhill	31	28			1	74
Ludgershall	35	18			5	64
Perham Box		31				
Tidworth	2	15				
Collingbourne	37	55			8	21
Collingbourne Kingston	38	79			9	45
Grafton	41	75			12	41
Grafton South Jc.	42	67			13	33
Grafton East Jc.		44				
Wolfhall Jc.		42				
Savernake	44	1	44	10	14	47 (H.L.)
Marlborough	48	78	49	29	19	44
Ogbourne	53	45	53	76	24	11
Chiseldon Camp	55	74	56	25	26	40
Chiseldon	57	10	57	41	27	56
Swindon Town	60	21	60	52	30	67
Rushey Platt	61	78	62	29	32	44
Rushey Platt GWR Jc.		33				
Swindon GWR	1	18				
Moredon	64	33	64	64	34	79
Blunsdon	66	12	66	43	36	58
Cricklade	68	48	68	79	39	14
Cerney	72	4	72	35	42	50
Cirencester	75	14	75	45	45	60
Foss Cross	81	26	82	57	51	72
Chedworth	82	45	83	76	53	11
Chedworth Woods Sdg.	84	62	85	13	55	28
Withington	86	8	86	39	56	54
Dowdeswell	88	26	88	57	58	72
Andoversford	88	76	89	27	59	42
Charlton Kings	92	53	93	8		
Cheltenham S. and Leckhampton	93	67	94	18		
Gloucester Loop Jc.	95	18	95	49		
Lansdown Jc.	95	67	96	18		
Cheltenham Lansdown	96	4	96	35		
Cheltenham High St.	96	69	97	20		

4: STATIONS AND HALTS

	Opened (Passengers)	Closed (Passengers)	
Weyhill	1.5.82	11.9.61	
Ludgershall	1.5.82	11.9.61	
Collingbourne Kingston Halt	1.4.32	11.9.61	
Collingbourne	1.5.82	11.9.61	Goods closed same date
Grafton	1.5.82	11.9.61	Goods closed same date
Savernake H.L.	26.6.98	15.9.58	Goods closed 22.6.59
Marlborough L.L.	27.7.81	11.9.61	Coal depot only from 19.5.64; closed entirely 7.9.64
Ogbourne	27.7.81	11.9.61	Goods closed same date
Chiseldon Camp Halt	1.12.30	11.9.61	
Chiseldon	27.7.81	11.9.61	Goods closed same date
Swindon Town	27.7.81	11.9.61	From 19.5.64 handled coal-class traffic and oil tanks for Esso only From 1.11.66 handles oil tanks only (Esso) on a private siding basis
Rushey Platt	18.12.83	1.10.05	
Moredon Platform	25.3.13	28.9.24	
Blunsdon	1.9.95	28.9.24	Weekday passenger service ceased from 10.7.22; Sunday service from 28.9.24 Goods closed 1.8.37
Cricklade	18.12.83	11.9.61	Goods closed 1.7.63
South Cerney	18.12.83	11.9.61	Goods closed 1.7.63
Cirencester	18.12.83	11.9.61	Goods closed 1.4.64
Foss Cross	1.8.91	11.9.61	Goods closed same date
Chedworth	1.10.92	11.9.61	Unstaffed halt from 1.2.54
Withington	1.8.91	11.9.61	Unstaffed halt from 28.5.56; closed to goods 28.5.56
Andoversford and Dowdeswell	1.8.91	1.4.27	Goods closed 15.10.62
Tidworth	1.10.02	19.9.55	Goods closed 25.11.55

5: MSW LOCOMOTIVES

Class and number	Wheel arrangement	Builder	Year
Purchased by Swindon, Marlborough & Andover Railway			
A 1 (30)	0—6—0T	Dübs	1881
2	0—6—0T	,,	1881
3	0—6—0T	,,	1881
B 4	0—4—4T	Avonside (?)	1878
C 5	2—4—0T	Beyer Peacock	1882
6	2—4—0T	,,	1882
7	2—4—0T	,,	1882
D 8 (29)	2—4—0T	,,	1884
Purchased by Midland & South Western Junction Railway			
E 9	4—4—0	Dübs	1893
G 10	2—4—0	,,	1894
11	2—4—0	,,	1894
12	2—4—0	,,	1894
F 13	0—6—0T	,,	1894
4 (14)	0—6—0T	,,	1894
H 14	2—6—0	Beyer Peacock	1895
I 15	0—4—4T	,,	1895
H 16	2—6—0	,,	1897
J 17	4—4—4T	Sharp Stewart	1897
18	4—4—4T	,,	1897
K 19	0—6—0	Beyer Peacock	1899
20	0—6—0	,,	1899
21	0—6—0	,,	1899
22	0—6—0	,,	1899
23	0—6—0	,,	1899
24	0—6—0	,,	1899
25	0—6—0	,,	1902
26	0—6—0	,,	1902
27	0—6—0	,,	1902
28	0—6—0	,,	1902
L 1	4—4—0	North British	1905
2	4—4—0	,,	1909
3	4—4—0	,,	1909
4	4—4—0	,,	1914
5	4—4—0	,,	1912
6	4—4—0	,,	1910
7	4—4—0	,,	1911
8	4—4—0	,,	1912
31	4—4—0	,,	1914

Diameter of coupled wheels ft	in	Cylinders	Tractive effort	Year withdrawn
4	0	15½ x 22	11,200	1916
4	0	15½ x 22	11,200	1906
4	0	15½ x 22	11,200	1906
5	6	16 x 22	10,115 (?)	1892
5	6	16 x 24	9,500	1912
5	6	16 x 24	9,500	1906
5	6	16 x 24	9,500	1910
5	6	17 x 24	11,025	1918
6	0	17 x 24	13,920	1924
5	6	17 x 24	13,399	1952
5	6	17 x 24	13,399	1952
5	6	17 x 24	13,399	1954
4	7	17 x 24	17,195	1926
4	7	17 x 24	17,195	1926
4	0	18 x 26	20,884	1914
5	2	17 x 24	13,312	1930
4	0	18 x 26	20,884	1930
5	3	17 x 24	14,972	1927
5	3	17 x 24	14,972	1929
5	2½	18 x 26	17,185	1936
				1934
				1938
				1934
				1937
				1936
				1935
				1934
				1937
				1937
5	9	18 x 26	16,603	1935
				1931
				1936
				1935
				1938
				1935
				1932
				1938
				1935

Acknowledgements and Bibliography

Valuable assistance has been received from the staff of the BRB Archives; from the sr Civil Engineer; from I. E. Gray, Gloucestershire Records Office; from M. G. Rathbone, Wiltshire Records Office; and the Public Records Office. I also owe thanks to the Librarians of Cheltenham Public Libraries and of Swindon Public Library.

The editors of the *Andover Advertiser*, the *Marlborough Times* and the *Wilts & Glos Standard* kindly allowed me to use their files.

J. H. Scholes, custodian of the BRB's transport relics, has been most helpful, and Messrs Beyer Peacock Gorton Ltd, Metropolitan-Cammell Ltd and the Colonel Commanding 1 Railway Group RCT have provided some elusive technical data. Enthusiasts and former employees have taken much trouble to help me, and I must particularly thank the following: Messrs Sid Baker, A. J. Ball, C. Barlow, H. Bint, S. Butler, R. Carpenter, G. Coates, W. Cripps, C. Curtiss, J. Davies, R. J. Dewey, F. Gale, R. P. Gardiner, J. A. Gould, L. Hoskins, D. L. Houldridge, D. J. Hyde, R. Hyde, T. Jenkins, F. Jones, S. P. Johnstone, L. B. Lapper, L. H. Leedham, Newcombe, R. Parker, A. Reed, A. Roberts; Rev C. A. Selman; Messrs M. Smith, W. Teal, B. Wheeler, M. Wigmore, A. Wilkins, I. Wood.

C. R. Clinker should have especial thanks for checking the manuscript.

Transcripts of Crown Copyright records in the Public Record Office appear by permission of the Controller of HM Stationery Office.

The following are among the books and periodicals consulted:

E. L. Ahrons, *Locomotive and Train Working in the latter part of the Nineteenth Century*. Vol. IV. 1953.

G. Behrend, *Gone With Regret*. 1964.

E. F. Carter, *Britain's Railway Liveries*. 1952.

C. R. Clinker, *Register of Closed Passenger Stations and Goods Depots in England*. Vol. II, 1900-1964. 1964.

H. Ellis, *Nineteenth Century Railway Carriages in the British Isles*. 1949.

C. Hadfield, *The Canals of Southern England*. 1955.

S. H. P. Higgins, *The Wantage Tramway*. 1958.

E. T. MacDermot, *History of the Great Western Railway*. 1927.

C. F. D. Marshall, *A History of the Southern Railway*. 2nd edition, revised by R. W. Kidner. 1963.

H. W. Paar, *A History of the Railways of the Forest of Dean*: Part 1, *The Severn & Wye Railway*. 1963.

Railway Correspondence & Travel Society, *Locomotives of the Great Western Railway*, Part 10. 1966.
T. B. Sands, *The Midland & South Western Junction Railway*. 1959.
Victoria History of Wiltshire, Vol. IV. 1959.
H. P. White, *Regional History of the Railways of Great Britain*: Vol. II, *Southern England*. 1964.

Index To Local & Personal Acts, 1801-1947. 1949.

Newspapers and periodicals: *The Engineer, Engineering, The Locomotive, Model Railway News, Railway Chronicle, Railway Magazine, Railway Observer, Railway Times, Bradshaw, Illustrated London News, Andover Advertiser, Cheltenham Examiner, Cheltenham Free Press, Gloucestershire Echo, Marlborough Times, North Wilts Herald, Swindon Advertiser, Wilts & Glos Standard*.

ILLUSTRATIONS

The author would like to thank the following for permission to use their photographs:
Messrs Beyer Peacock, 19, 20, 21; British Railways, 32, 38, 40, 41, 42; S. Butler, 24; H. C. Casserley, 23; W. Cripps, 12; J. Gould, 48; S. C. Nash, 47; Locomotive & General Railway Photographs, 11, 34, 43, 45; Locomotive Publishing Company, 17, 18, 25; P. J. T. Reed, 26, 28; Real Photographs Co., 22, 27, 29, 30, 31, 33, 35, 36, 37, 39; A. Roberts, 1, 7; R. C. Riley, 2, 6, 8.
The remaining photographs were taken by the author.

Index

Illustrations are indicated by heavy type